Million Dollar Broker

THE COMMERCIAL REAL ESTATE SENSATION

Change your life, change your perspective on wealth, and give you and your family what you've always dreamed of.

Scott W Johnstone
Founder *of* Commercial Real Estate Brokers Academy
www.commercialrealestatebrokersacademy.com

Commercial
Real Estate
Brokers Academy

Liability

No responsibility or liability is assumed or accepted by the author for any claimed financial losses and/or damages sustained to persons from the use of the information in this publication, personal or otherwise, directly or indirectly. While every effort has been made to ensure the reliability and accuracy of the information within, all liability, negligence or otherwise, from any use, misuse or abuse of the operation of any methods, strategies, instructions or ideas contained in the material herein, is the sole responsibility of the reader. By reading past this point, you are accepting these terms and conditions.

Dedicated to my late grandmother, Marilynn P. Ellis, author, poet, artist, and the best mother anyone could ever have. She taught me passion, courage, and unconditional love. She saved my life and led me to be a great father, leader, and lover of all that's beautiful, and the man I hope to be.

Contents

Introduction

This book is dedicated to changing your life by teaching you to become one of the top one percent of money earners in the country. While living a purposeful, fulfilling life, you can give you and your family the lifestyle you all dream of. I know from personal experience that by following these proven strategies, you *can* change your life forever.

Packed with these strategies and tactics, this book provides information previously inaccessible to anyone outside of the top brokerage firms. The once secretive, closed fraternity of commercial real estate is now open to anyone. Regardless of your gender, race, family background, prior job experience, and education – you too can become a top commercial real estate broker.

Our society is in the middle of the greatest redistribution of knowledge and wealth in world history. Those of us who are determined to change stations in life can ride this unprecedented wave of opportunity by learning the insider secrets that, until now, have been hidden behind the corporate walls of top commercial real estate brokerage firms.

You can fulfill your calling in life, and become the person you are meant to be. You can obtain financial freedom for you and your family, eventually allowing more time for the passions in your life. You'll have the ability to give back to society, thus leaving a lasting legacy for both you and your family. In the final appraisal, your life will have mattered.

If this sounds far-fetched or hard to believe, it is also the unvarnished truth. I am living proof that anyone in America or elsewhere, who has a basic education, tremendous desire and tenacity, and lives in or around a commercial business hub, can earn $1 million per year in gross commissions in the commercial real estate industry. You can do all this while earning the respect of your family, community leaders, and most importantly, yourself.

Who or what is a commercial real estate broker and why use one? Commercial agents and brokers have provided commercial real estate solutions for facilities such as office, warehouse, retail locations, and others, since before the industrial revolution. They've helped both small and large companies, ranging from the mom and pop store, to members of the Fortune Five Hundred.

Brokers are industry specialists who represent proprietors, tenants, and investors in all their commercial sales and leasing needs. Their indepth and timely market knowledge, coupled with their knowledge of various commercial deal structures, enable them to negotiate the best possible terms for their clients. Often, this literally translates to saving or making clients millions in a single transaction. Brokers best represent their clients when they figuratively become part of their corporate team, to provide strategic and tactical advantages that accomplish both financial and operational goals.

A good broker provides a friendly but unrelenting advocacy for their clients. Not only do they serve as advocates for their clients, they also serve as buffers between opposing parties who have a vested interest in maintaining long lasting relationships. Additionally, during the heated battle during negotiations for deals in the millions or billions of dollars, the broker leverages the valuable time of the company officers, allowing them to focus on their core business.

Brokers act as trusted advisors to owners or investors to help grow their portfolios, as well as mitigate losses, all the while earning a great living in good times or bad. They also assist retailers in finding the perfect location so their first ventures into business are successful. The advantages a broker provides are innumerable just like any great business leader.

The commercial brokerage industry of the past has been made up of nearly exclusively white males that had been recommended into one of the major firms, and had gone through extensive training programs lasting one to two years, and covering all types of disciplines within the business. Brokers usually are from a local major university and from one of the most powerful fraternities. Alternatively, they are usually brought into the business by a family member who's a "legacy" in the industry.

The top firms like competitive athletes and risk-takers for their competitive spirit and entrepreneurial predisposition. One major firm not only puts you through a series of interviews with brokers, managers and executives of the company but they also enroll you into an eight hour psychological battery of tests to determine whether if you match a psychological role mode based on the profiles of previously successful brokers.

If you're finally hired, you become a trainee in the research department learning the basics macroeconomic drivers of the business, while simultaneously allowing senior brokers to get to know you. You are then considered for what is normally called a "Runnership" program.

A "Runnership" program lasts between one and two years and it is based on the notion that the best way to learn is though immersion with a senior broker for a lengthy period of time, and that this immersion in your mentor's daily routine will teach you the finer points of the business.

The duties of a new "Runner" are typically copying, packaging, binding, cold calling and attending meetings & presentations. Runners do not participate at this stage, as typically trainers have a "listen but don't speak" policy, until much later in your training.

During the "Runnership", or indentured servitude, your aim is to bond with your trainer and learn as much as possible. This will later allow you to be successful on your own and make your millions. During training, the typical pay is $24,000 per year, for the one to two years it takes to earn your stripes and complete your training. This level of income is barely above the poverty line and most people who go through it require the financial and moral support of family or loved ones, who help bridge the financial gap.

Ideally, the trainer has taught them the finer points of the industry, and has Imparted the skills and wisdom. They hope the acquired knowledge, as well as creating relationships that will allow the runner to stay afloat out on their own. In appreciation for a job well done often the runner is invited to join the trainer in a partnership.

The average early stage tenured broker for one of the top five firms in the nation, on average, earn gross commissions of $1.1 million annually. Those gross commissions are then split with the house and paid out to the broker, after further splits with partners, if any. The top leading brokers in the top five firms average $3.6 million in gross commissions annually and also split their commissions accordingly.

You may not have been born into the "right family" or gone to the "right" school or university but you have something that previous generations of prospective brokers never had. You have the Internet. All the data ever needed to succeed are at your fingertips. The step-by-step process of becoming a world-class broker offered to you through online training and this book. You have several series of audio and video training courses from world-class experts. Subscription-based online data service companies provide all the research and property data provided, only a select few in major firms previously had access to this in the past. Thanks to these expanded opportunities for self training, firms are willing to take you on with less human training, more virtual learning, and shorter or no "Runnership" campaigns.

The world economy has made a fundamental shift toward paying the highest incomes to business leaders, who can provide knowledge, process, and execution in specific fields that include commercial real estate. Today's knowledge and process based pay is disproportionate to the amount of money paid in the old "time for money model," in which the worker is paid on an hourly scale. Time-for-money never allows workers a chance to get ahead of the financial curve. Today's contact, knowledge, and process-driven pay that commercial brokers receive, allows for the community to be served at the highest level while providing the Broker a world class lifestyle enjoyed only by the top 1% of earners in the nation.

I feel it's my life's mission to inform those in our society who are looking for a start or a change. I'm talking about a change that will provide true peace of mind to all of the hard working individuals out there looking to change their station in life, give back to the community, and give their families what they never had growing up. I'm not talking just about material things, I'm talking about things like the best education for your children, money for retirement, a home wherever you choose, and respect from your peers, your community and your loved ones.

You see, I came from humble beginnings, and encountered some tough times when I was young I was far from privileged. My tough times started early, and I didn't make it easier on myself by being a rebel and a "bad" kid. I saw what I didn't want for my life and I was lucky enough to change it. I was blessed by a few people who gave me a shot at being a better person. I want to give that blessing to you, but you know what they say, "luck is the residue of hard work," so if you're ready to give it the effort, and work hard and smart, then I'm willing to show you how to become The Million-Dollar Broker.

Chapter One

The Secret Handshake of the Commercial Real Estate Broker

It's February 2010. We're in the biggest recession since the great depression. I look across the room of the banquet hall on "fight night" and instantly notice the nods and winks from the seasoned vets, and the boyish zeal of the rookies. They're smoking cigars and cheering on the two boxers beating the hell out of each other – all for the entertainment of the group of 600 industry attendees – who were decked out in black ties. As I mingle through the smoke filled room to line up for another cocktail – my belly full of filet mignon and asparagus, topped off with fine red wine – I've no other thought than to fill my glass before last call. At the same time, a group of the top 20 to 40 guys are all headed to an after dinner spot where the single guys will meet up with the model hostesses that were hired to dress up the room by the event leaders that night. The married guys will show up as well to watch the games begin, while the ladies all vie for the highest status guys and the guys all play the game to do the same but status is less of a concern to the boys than beauty and sex appeal.

Before we can get there, however, the lines of Mercedes and the occasional Maserati or Bentley have to be brought to their rightful owner. Those brave or dumb enough to drive after drinking, do so willingly – as this is a group of high-level risk takers, most of which were seasoned athletes. In addition, they all believe, to some degree, that they are invincible, or at least while the vodka is still streaming through their veins. The destination is a place well known for those in "the know" on Pacific Coast Highway, with a band of high-level young brokers who are on a mission to find a mate or at least a mate that night.

A solid stream of S and SL class Mercedes Benz roll up to the after party spot. Upon arrival, the valet gives everyone the "secret handshake," as he knows most of them by name.

This is a well-known spot for young brokers -- many of whom make their own hours so they can choose to come in when they feel the need. Their only real bosses are their clients, and most of them are with their broker. The truth of the matter is that their clients were probably one of them not long ago and might have even trained the young bucks back in the day, as this small community of insiders is incredibly close nit.

"He's a great guy." This is something you hear occasionally about people in the business and definitely something you *want* to hear frequently about yourself. Unfortunately, more often than not, you might hear a terrible story of a mistake someone made, as it can also be an industry of sharks, vying for position by knocking their competition, in order to better their position in the eyes of the small group of the important decision makers.

Now most of the rest of the group that night, the seasoned vets, have taken the high road and found their way home by cab or learned their lesson years earlier not to go big and hurt yourself that night, as this is just another night.

Your clients will respect you tomorrow just as they had the day before. These old dogs have learned to do the right thing. That is, by coming home to their wives and kids at a reasonable hour, telling the story of the night *exactly* as it happened. The wife already knows that the perfume she smells is that of the hostess coming in for a test probe to see what kind of guy he really is. He is the guy mentioned earlier. "He's a great guy!" He is reliable and honest, trustworthy and candid, self-assured but not cocky. He might drive the nearly mandatory Mercedes, but it's way beyond its warranty and he owns it free and clear, just as he owns his house and boat that rests in the bay, visible from his balcony up on the hill. This is the last thing he'll see before he kisses his kids goodnight.

Afterward, he settles in for a good night's sleep so he can hit the office early in the morning to ensure he gets a jump on his day by leaving messages for all the hung-over young bucks he's doing deals with that haven't made it out of bed yet.

The young guys will still make gross commissions on average this year of over $500,000, a decent year in a bad economy, but the seasoned vets will quietly clear more than $2,000,000 as the extra effort and focus a loving family brings makes all the difference. They are calmer, don't have as much to prove and are less focused than the younger guys on issues of status. Their focus is on making their lives the best they can be for their loved ones, their wives, daughters and sons, and those in their immediate families, that need the help to carry on with pride and honor, intelligence and dignity.

The mission of these community leaders is to make their life worth living and to do it with purpose and drive. They usually are involved in the community, reaching out to those less fortunate than they are, in the process making themselves better people, all the while keeping their eye on the prize, the prize being the love and respect of their family.

The story I just told you is true. The "great guy" I refer to is real. I won't mention his name, but he is very close to me, and I know him and his family intimately. I grew up in the business with him and we have lived our lives in this industry for more than 25 years. His story isn't uncommon, as there are thousands of guys just like him in this little known industry of experts in commercial real estate. We are paid for our knowledge and our process, making millions for our clients, and are paid a percentage of every deal we close, not an hourly wage. This expertise has been passed down the line to us from generation to generation of experts.

That has been the way since the great earthquake of 1906 when Colbert Coldwell met Benjamin Arthurs and formed the greatest commercial real estate firm in history from the ashes of downtown San Francisco. Now the secrets of the industry are opening up to anyone that can access it and make sense of it and has the courage to take the leap. Before now you had to be born into the right family with the right connections, have attended the right college or been in the right fraternity. The list of silver-spoon kids in the industry is long.

Enter the age of the Internet, with open platforms of information and online, subscription based access to all the data one ever needs to be the best the industry has ever seen. Enter the online training experts who, for a small price, will give you the step-by-step processes of how to become one of the best in the industry. By simply combining the rules of the industry with their own hard work ethic, in a very short period of time, they'll make more money than they ever expected by closing deals in their community. All the while making lasting relationships with the leaders of industry in the community and enriching their lives with invaluable life experiences.

These open platforms of information are allowing for a diversity of people to enter the industry either on their own or with brokerage companies looking for volume through masses. It's an exciting time for women, minorities, and underprivileged in the industry as the old-boy networks are now less relevant than knowledge, work ethic, honesty, character, diligence, enthusiasm, skill, insight, strategy and tactic. Less and less are we judged by last names as is the past.

This is the good news for all those brave enough to take on the challenge of changing your station in life, building a wealth of knowledge to use to better increase your income, increase your free time, choose who your boss is and make your own hours.

The bad news is that the information may be there but the lessons of the ages seem to be lacking. Some moral and ethical rules are left out; as a result, some new age brokers might think this is a fast buck, get rich quick solution to the woes of our nation's economic meltdown. The reality is that anything worth doing in life is worth doing well. Without the mentoring and lessons learned from those who have come before, the new economy broker may fail before he gets off the ground when faced with adversity or the ethical teachings of those who have come before him.

It's easy to make money in this industry when times are good it's the measure of how well someone is trained when they are able to prosper in the down times like the example of my "good guy "friend I spoke of earlier in this chapter.

The recent lending crisis and subsequent massive job losses within the mortgage industry have created a mass migration of new age brokers who have come over to commercial real estate brokerage from mortgage lending; with them have also come the bad habits of the mortgage lending industry which up until recently was all about churning through as many deals as possible with little or no qualification of the client. Unfortunately, those individuals who bring the mortgage lending mentality to commercial real estate typically die on the vine with such a mindset. The commercial brokerage industry and the clients we serve are typically extremely conservative in their approach to business and have the long game in mind while managing transactions. What I mean by long game is the "big picture" to doing business, building relationships in the industry, and serving their community and families.

If you wouldn't do the deal yourself then you should never recommend it to your clients or potential clients. This is the gut check one has to consider prior to giving any advice or recommendations. Make no mistake, our clients are looking to us for solid, ethical, intelligent advice, as we are typically the connection to the information on the street level. If you've been in the business long enough you're now possibly the "wisdom" in the room given your historical perspective and this is even more valuable to clients so the "go slow and make a good decision" approach is more of what is required to make it in this business.

Too many get rich quick thinkers have come into commercial brokerage in the past ten years with information learned about the mechanics of the industry from lack of good training from these open platforms of information, online trainers, and data delivery services. Not enough of them have come into the business with the right mental attitude towards fellow brokers, clients, and vendors. Additionally not enough psychological and social method has been brought to the industry by the trainers and it's time for a change.

Too many get rich quick guys have made too many ethical mistakes and have said, "I'll take the money and deal with the consequences later," no matter what damage they do to coworkers, clients, their firms, and their own reputations. They can do a deal but they wreak havoc in the process, as they haven't learned the lessons of the past and haven't received training to make good decisions. It's time for a change.

In the next coming years of the commercial brokerage business, the ones who will win are those who are the long game thinkers. The one's whose moral compass is always pointing "North." The ones who will win in the future are those who are more collaborative, have high integrity and authenticity, are more approachable, and are visible leaders in the community. The ones who will succeed in the end are those who have been taught the wisdom of the past while embracing the technological advances of today and the future.

The ones who will lose in the future are those upstarts who haven't learned the moral and ethical lessons of the past, as well as those older "dinosaurs" who haven't embraced the potential that technology and the internet brings. Those who are stuck in the past or those who are in the present but don't have the historical lessons vital so not to repeat the mistakes from generations that have come before them are in trouble.

How did I come to these conclusions? The reason is that I have witnessed the way the business used to be and how it has evolved and I have had to evolve with it. I came from the wrong family and from the wrong side of the tracks and through hard work and determination, succeeded in this very elite business.

I was trained old school at two of the biggest firms in the world. I lived through the technological advances the industry has benefited from. I've worked alongside and been subject to the influx of the get rich quick thinkers and the havoc they create. I have evolved with my own companies as only a small business owner can because it's make–or–break time, all the time.

I have been on top for the better part of 25 years in this business and know the most up to date techniques, strategies, tactics, and formulas for success, as well as the moral and ethical lessons of the past. I've trained, mentored, and partnered with some of the best in the business and they have all gone on to live the lives of their dreams. Join me and let me help you do the same.

Chapter Two

My Personal Story and My Passion for Overcoming the Odds

I'm an eight-year-old, toe head blond kid in late summer of 1969. I'm sunburned from the beach in Santa Monica in my grandparents 1913, Glendale hills home. Peacefully enjoying my evening, pre-bed, bath session with Mr. Bubble and my rubber duck, a World War II flotilla and Aqua Man, I have not a care in the world when my grandmother uncharacteristically barges in, visibly shaken and welling up with tears. She asks me if she can talk to me about something.

Now I'm eight and that's right about the age when you don't want your Grandma or any other woman hovering over you, naked, bubbles fading and water getting colder by the minute, asking to talk about anything, but she's my world as mom and dad are out of the picture so I say "Ok, Grandma, what?"

"Your mother is about to ruin your life!" I wasn't aware of it at the time, but my mom and dad had done some serious damage to my young life. For example, they were seventeen and senior's in high school when they had me. Evidently, condoms weren't available to my 17-year-old dad when they did "it" at the local drive-in on their first date. My parent's marriage came about because my maternal grandfather was a devout Catholic, so having an abortion was out of the question. Between this time and when I was born, my now absent father entered the Navy and was based out of Oakland; he moved us to the San Francisco bay area onto the naval barracks. After my dad ruffed up my mom a couple times, my great grandmother drove 16 hours round trip to the bay area to retrieve my brother, my mother, and myself from the guy who started this mess.

So we're back to the bathtub. "She's going to ruin your life!" I'm thinking 'huh? what do you mean?' So I say, "why are you crying

Grandma?" She said, "Your mom is breaking off her engagement to Chuck (her boss) and she's now going to marry this Hispanic gentleman, an ex- convict out of San Quentin Prison, a heroin dealer and they want to move you boys to east Los Angeles.

So for those who don't know east LA, it's known as the barrio for most of LA's Mexican street gangs. Therefore, it doesn't take a genius to figure out that East LA isn't the place for a toe head, blond, skinny white kid to show his face. After all, the badass locals would literally eat me alive, beat the shit out of me daily, and eventually turn me into either a white version of them, or kill me.

So my Grandma in very graphic detail explains all this to me and I start balling my eyes out not only for the fear factor but because I really don't want to move away from her and the life I have. You have to understand, my grandmother was the sweetest woman you could ever hope to meet. She was cum lade at Penn State and a terrific artist, poet, song writer, wonderful cook, and the person who kept us on the right track. She fed us and told us the best bed time stories ever – where we were always the hero's. Most importantly, she gave us the biggest gift of all – unconditional love. So moving away from her with my now 26-year-old flakey mom with her new drug dealing husband from the barrios of east LA to who knows where, scared the hell out of me and made bath time a traumatic, crying session filled with fear and anxiety I'll never forget.

So flash forward a bit. Rather than move to the barrio, my grandparents bought a modest house for my mom and stepdad in a decent neighborhood some 20 miles away in Burbank where the Disney studios are. The marriage was filled with violence, strife, and visits to the barrio on "family" gatherings. It also included fights to defend my younger brother, as well as myself, plus lessons on how to saw off shotguns, hide in the bushes from local gangs, and all around survival techniques that no nine-year-old should ever be required to learn. After enough physical abuse, visits to the local minimum-security prisons to visit my step dad, stabbings, and unannounced visits from the local police, my mom figured out that this was a bad guy and divorced him.

Unfortunately, this meant I had to step in to be the surrogate father for my now two younger brothers while my mom was out looking for a new man. This meant we survived off $100 a week, basically living off MacDonald's and whatever I could cook at fourteen. Needless to say, I was pissed all the time as school became second to survival. By the time I was 15 and a sophomore in high school, I was expelled to continuation school for a prank where I put dry ice in my math teachers back pocket. One week into high school and I was summarily dismissed to where the other abandoned kids and misfits went to "learn on their own schedule."

One day an incident where, fed up with it all, I dowsed my mom with a glass of milk for who knows what and that was it. "You're going to live with your father." 'Oh, shit' I thought. Out of the frying pan and into the fire. Now you have to realize, even though my mom made questionable decisions about men, I still loved her. Even though she'd been absent a lot I still needed her in my life. And all I knew of my dad was from spending week long visits with him during the summers in dreary Portland, Oregon. He would wake us up to revelry every morning and pour cold water on us if we weren't up by 7:00 sharp (during summer vacation!) Now if you were a normal kid you remember that the best part of summer vacation was sleeping in until whenever you felt like. This guy took great pleasure in the agony we felt, I'm sure channeling his navy days, where his C.O. or military father did to him. Well, we were around five and seven years old at the time and it left a distinct memory of the kind of guy he was and the idea of being shipped off to this man was almost as scary as moving in with Mr. San Quentin.

So, after a year-and-a-half of being told I was evil and living as an indentured servant, along with a few physical confrontations and being knocked around- I called my mom and told her I would be the best kid ever if she would please take me back. Indeed, five days later, I was on a plane home, back to sunny southern California.

Shortly after we moved back in with my grandparents because my mom proved once again to be an unfit mother. We were back in bliss at Grandma's: unconditional love, three square meals a day, a ride to water polo practice at 6:00 am, and good grades - all because we simply were able to focus on being kids and good students which gained us the respect of our classmates and teachers.

This was my senior year in high school and although I pulled it together – water polo and swim team, good grades, my coaches' and math teachers' Teaching Assistants, great social life, home on time, and the dream of becoming a doctor, it still wasn't enough to overcome the three previous disastrous years of mediocre grades. Therefore, my chances of entering a university were shot.

So what came next was an odd surprise. A plan either devised by my grandmother or an altruistic move on my dad's part came in the form of a phone call from my at the time estranged father, inviting me to come live with him in Eugene Oregon to attend Lane Community Junior College with the plan of eventually transferring to the University of Oregon. So with no other plan or opportunities, after graduation and with much trepidation I set off for Oregon again.

The deal wasn't quite as good as presented as my tuition, room and board in his home was paid for but books, car, clothes gas, etc. was my responsibility so I quickly found a job, enrolled as a Biology major as the Dr. calling was still in me and I was off to college. To avoid conflict and confrontation I spent as much time on campus as possible. From early in the morning to dark I was either in class, studying or involved in sports, mainly volleyball, as swimming wasn't much of a sport in Oregon, too rainy I guess.

I put in my two years and just as I was about to transfer to the University of Oregon, my dad announced to me that he, his wife, and new son we moving off to Portland. Now, Portland was three hours away and if I wanted to continue to be supported with room, board, and tuition, I'd have to change my plan and move with them and attend a little known collage named Portland State University, which just happened to be where my dad graduated. It would be a great thing, according to him. Well that might have been a good deal for him but to me I had been busting my hump to go to the University of Oregon, as planned and had for two years been getting to know the town and the people etc. to this end. Moving to some new city simply to follow my dad's life plan was not appealing. However, as I didn't have the funds to venture out on my own, I went along.

Once again, long story short, I was in a new, unfamiliar town with no friends and a campus and staff I never was properly introduced to by my preoccupied "parents." Things just did not work out. All the while, I still had to have a job to pay for my car, clothes, social life, etc. so I lasted about a week at this new school and all I could think of was that I was wasting valuable time in my life as this just wasn't working out.

So a new plan came to me. I'll take on more hours at work, save a few bucks, and move back home. Take my chances and make a life for myself. So I did just that. I saved $830, contacted my younger brother living in Costa Mesa, California, a town in Orange County, California near Newport Beach. I said "Hey bro, I'm headed home and need to sleep on your couch for thirty days while I get a job and figure out what I'm gonna do with my life." He and his high school buddies weren't very thrilled about the idea as I was the big, mean senior when they were sophomores in high school and I pretty much hazed them all the time, but after pleading my case a couple times they said thirty days and that's it.

So I did just that and found a job in retail that paid the bills and was also doing the one thing I knew I could do which was sales, having done so in college to make ends meet. Another thing retail allowed me to do was to make commissions, which if I hustled more than the average employee, allowed me to make a decent living and live above the poverty line. So as soon as I got my first paycheck I thanked my brother and his roommates, bought them a case of beer and moved to an apartment a block off the beach and shared a room with a buddy I met who was looking to split the bills. We both had small single beds and both snored like hell but it was heaven compared to the couch and I was on my own in Newport Beach a block from the sand and the waves.

"So what's next for me," I thought? I had this burning desire to become more than a subsistence level retail guy. It's not that that's a bad thing, but for some reason, I had visions of grandeur. Maybe it was the stories my Grandma told me when I was a kid where I was always the hero. Or the trip where I ran away from home at fifteen for a month with a buddy to Wisconsin, where he was from, in late winter, where I saw the world as it really was: tough and hard and if you don't take action to better your station you'll be just another worker bee struggling to make ends meet. Now that scared the heck out of me and with my grandma's help in overinflating my ego I knew I could do anything I put my head and my heart into, no matter what the odds.

Now I wasn't stupid, I knew I had blown the whole Doctor thing and I knew I had to probably find a career in sales where I could get someone to give me a shot and teach me the ropes. I also knew that commission sales were what I was good at and that the higher the sales price the better, simple math. So I started looking around and meeting as many people as I could who were successful who might point me in the right direction. Enter three key people in my life. My girlfriend and two guys I happen to meet through friends that happen to both work for the same company which at the time was called "Coldwell Banker". The girlfriend introduced me to one and a girl I worked with at Nordstrom introduced me to the other. To this day, these guys are two of my best friends and I'd throw myself in front of a bus for them if it meant saving their lives.

The first guy named Bob sat me down and told me the inner workings of how to go about getting a job with his firm, which by the way was almost impossible for a guy like me. I had no diploma, no fraternity, no relative in the business but he recommended me to Paul, whom I had just happened to meet at a birthday party my girlfriend took me to. Now, it just happened Paul and I also had a conversation about the business at the party prior to Bob's and my talk, but he was a bit more reserved in his description as how to get a job as he was actually hiring a "Runner." His first "Runner", as it happened, and he was reading me as a prospect. In retrospect, it made all the sense in the world as when I would ask a question he would always come back with a question himself.

Well, I finally put two and two together and immediately called Paul. I said something to the effect of, if he would be willing to sit down and talk, I would make it worth his while, as he was never going to find anyone with more drive, tenacity, desire or raw talent than me. I needed someone like him on my team to help me get hired and show me the ropes. I went on to say that if he were to give me this chance he would have my undying loyalty for life and could treat me like a dog and I'd happily and willingly come back for more.

He asked me what I did and at the time I was selling menswear at Nordstrom. He said "Great, I need a new suit so I'll come in to see you this Thursday and see if you can help me find something suitable." Now I was the king of hustle at what I did so I couldn't be happier.

Well, Thursday came and Paul rolls up, right on time and dressed to the nines. He said, "I'm not sure this store has anything that is my style." Paul was more of a fine Italian suit guy and Nordi's at the time was a bit more conservative so I went about qualifying his tastes and finding out what he had in his wardrobe and then went about filling in the holes as every well healed man has to have at least the basics.

Two hours later Paul left with six new suits, five new shirts, eight new ties, two new pairs of shoes, socks etc. etc. All the while, we really got to know each other and came to find that we came from somewhat similar backgrounds and I could tell he liked my tenacity and work ethic and I really liked his brutal candor.

He laid it out for me as clear as a bell. If I wanted a job I had to go through no less than eight interviews, and an eight-hour physiological test and then had to be recommended in by at least two current brokers that would vouch that I was a "good guy." He went on to say he already had a candidate ahead of me that he liked and that I would have to show him I could do a better job and make him more money than this other candidate, who by the way, went to the same fraternity as Paul.

So I go about scheduling the interviews and before every one Paul would prep me for what type of guy the interviewer was like. He likes this but not that. Wear this but not that. His favorite game is the NBA but don't bring up his wife and kids. Be blunt about your story of hard knocks but not too graphic. Emphasize your desire, tenacity, ability to learn fast, you're past sales experience and relate it somehow to commercial real estate. Always be completely honest, never puff, be humble but stick up for yourself, and tell him if he goes with you, it will be one of the best decisions he's ever made.

I can't say enough about Paul. The guy virtually gave me the roadmap, pointed out the roadblocks, mentored me through the process and when it came time to make a decision between me and the other guy took me on a little ride in his car. He basically had the green light to hire either of us and I knew he had already had this talk with the other candidate and the little ride we took was through our territory to get my opinion of what I knew of commercial real estate.

First of all the car we were in was his bright red Porsche Cabriolet and we were driving by an old Orange grove where a backhoe was plucking trees out of the ground like a kid would pick weeds while doing his chores. I turned to Paul and said what the heck are they doing to those poor trees. He said something I'll never forget. "Kid, you're gonna make millions off that land. By the way, you got the job and you start when we open our new office in two weeks." He said "you and me, we're the first hired, so we get a head start. Don't let me down."

I could hardly contain myself. In fact, I think I hugged the guy and did like 10 fist pumps because someone in my life finally saw something in me that I always knew myself and gave me a shot. Now to tell the truth I really had no idea what I was getting myself into. I was working for a great retailer at the time and my $20-35,000 was pretty much automatic as long as I showed up and hustled but this was a totally new experience. I had absolutely no business training. The pay for Runners at the time was $12,400 annually, with a small $200 gas allowance, which, by the way, living in Newport Beach or for that matter Nome Alaska was far below the poverty level, so I had to come up with a solution.

Enter my girlfriend. She and I had been paying for two separate apartments but really living in one. We had been going out for a year or so and there was either the choice for me to go find a couple guy roommates or take the plunge and move in together. Now she had a roommate and that was cool with her because she liked the idea of a guy around for protection but was I ready to do this? This meant the potential of marriage and I was only 23 years old at the time. I loved her so I said to myself what the hell; let's give it a shot.

So my first day at work I was scared to death. I had no idea what to expect and really no idea what I was doing. Thank God I had Paul reassuring me that if I just listened to him and didn't say anything stupid I'd get through training and be on my way to making my fortune. One thing I was able to convince Paul and my other interviewers was that because of my sales skills and experience that I could definitely make it through the training program in just a year and not the usual two-year program.

So I show up for my first day and hour early and couldn't even get in the building. I waited in my car until the office manager who was the nicest lady, greeted me and helped me fill out all the appropriate paperwork and get settled into my workstation or at the time they called them cubes, because that's what they were. Six foot by six foot cubes with a little storage space for files a phone and that's about it. But let me tell you that cube was my castle. I was the happiest guy on the planet. Behind me were the days of retail and ahead the promise of a real career where I'd have the opportunity to work with the top CEO's and leaders of the community and become a fraternity brother in the biggest Brokerage firm in the nation.

Well the next year was one of the most brutal of my life. I'd be in the office at 6:00 a.m. and out no later than 7:30 p.m. When we had special projects or presentations the next day I would literally work until 2:00 am and then sleep under my desk with a book propping up my head as a pillow and back at it at the crack of dawn. One thing I knew was maybe I didn't have the pedigree but no one was going to outwork or out hustle me. The thing of it is that the business isn't brain surgery. It's a lot of facts and figures, mixed with client psychology, basic sales skills, business development, business processes, marketing, and closing deals. Being friendly and helpful to the senior guys goes a long way and you want to make a good reputation for yourself because eventually you're going to need the senior brokers to bring you into deals after your Runnership (that is if you've made a good impression) because this business is about interdependence. This is a fancy word for teaming to spread the work so you always have a consistent deal flow and not the spikes and dips the lone brokers' experience.

So fortunately I work hard enough to make a good reputation for myself I dig up enough deals to make my mentor, Paul some incremental income, free his time up to chase girls (he was single at the time), and have a bit of fun. Then comes a lucky cold call.

Back in the day we were called "Runner"s for a reason: we delivered proposals and documents because time was of the essence and there was no Fed-Ex. We didn't have fax machines, Internet, or color copiers. Our secretaries typed on those IBM Selectric Typewriters with three copies of carbon paper. We were in the dark ages, but you know the one thing that hasn't changed – cold calling. It's either done in person by walking buildings while introducing yourself to a decision maker or by phone, which was my specialty.

I was good at charming my way past the gatekeeper, receptionist, or personal assistants and always tried to get a hold of the CFO or equivalent. The reason being he's the guy responsible for the money and takes it very seriously. So one lucky day when the Gods were shining on me I got through to the right guy at the right time and sure enough he was about to sign a lease on a 110,000 square foot warehouse that they had been in for a 10 years but had no broker advising him on the market. I asked a few questions and sure enough, his landlord was taking him to the cleaners. I suggested we meet briefly to review a survey of all the alternatives that met his parameters, invited my mentor to the meeting and sure enough after a brief tour, we found a better building for about 20% less than his current owner was proposing.

To make a long story short we closed the deal, as I was only eight months into my training and my mentor was ecstatic and magnanimous enough to include me in on 20 percent of the commissions, which he absolutely did not have to do. My share of the deal was $47,000 and having been living in near poverty, to me that was a tremendous amount of money to receive all at one time.

So that's a big win but that's not it. I finish my one year training, ""Runner"ship" program, they throw me a big coming out on your own party, I get put on a couple small low income listings, which I was happy to be on but quickly realized it was really up to me to take what I learned and put it to work and get it done. If I wanted the brass ring, I had to reach for it, and do it harder than I ever had as a "Runner". At this point, it was crunch time.

So I pulled out all the stops, cold called my ass off, met with every owner in my market, met with all the successful brokers to get any insight I might have missed. I drove every building in my market on weekends, took pictures, and built a database, which at the time was unheard of as there weren't even computers yet. Word, excel, Adobe, Google, Costar etc. were non-existent. Therefore, I had to invent the tools to make me the best in my market and make no mistake that was exactly my goal. Be the best or die trying. I wrote a newsletter and sent it to all the owners, tenants, banks and anyone who would listen because if they at least new my name and associated it with me being an expert then I could at least have a better chance of getting in the door which was half the battle.

At this point I'm half way through my rookie year with all the other first year guys. Basically, I'm competing to make the most money and therefore, earn a trophy saying "you're the best first year guy that year." More importantly, however, is the respect of the senior guys who might give me a shot of working together on a project and increasing my income.

So it's a Sunday night and I'm watching the local news and there's a story about a bank building burning down which just happens to be smack dab in the middle of my territory. To make things better I had just put together a market package of all the competitive buildings in the area together with statistics on available space, floor plans, photos, and an executive summary. It was perfect. All I had to do was to get to the office by 5:00 am, make 30 copies for all the tenants in the building coming to their burnt down building and have enough cards to hand out so I could be their broker and help find them a new home.

Now I'm not a fire engine chaser but to a young guy in the business it was perfect. I rolled up in my suit and acted like I owned the place, walked under the fire tape and into the bank branch offices and asked for the president of the bank. I briefly introduced myself and he says to me kid, you're exactly the person I need to talk to. For those who don't know banking rules, well those rules state that a bank can't close during normal operating hours for more than 24 hours and just like that, we were off to find him a new location.

Now you have to understand the bank wasn't the only tenant in the building. They were one of 30 other tenants and I was handing out cards and market studies like they were hotcakes. I was so busy I had to bring in two senior guys just to handle the paperwork and deal flow. That chain of events alone made me gross commissions of $250,000 that year and I still made over 20 other deals especially after I made a bit of a reputation for working hard and sharing the wealth. By the time my rookie year was over, I was far and away "Rookie of the Year" but also number four in the office out of 45 other brokers. Most of which were senior guys all wondering "how did this 24 year old kid do it?" So I chalked it all up to luck, dedication, desire, drive, my unrelenting passion for overcoming the odds and, of course, my trainer who gave me the knowledge to realize what to do when presented with an opportunity.

After all the fanfare of that year had faded my realization was: "You're only as good as your next deal." So I took some time to think about what I really wanted to be in this industry. Now one bit of information that will mean more to you later in the book is that I was trained as an "Industrial Broker." That means I worked on warehouses and R&D facilities with companies who had need for such facilities. I worked with manufacturers of nut's and bolts and high tech weaponry, clay pots, and widgets. Well that is a very specific vertical specialty and once you choose your field of expertise within the industry you usually never switch, simply because the time it takes to learn all the detail is so long that even considering making a change is daunting to say the least.

Because I had learned my craft in a newly developing market with rapid housing growth and lots of business migration, I was fortunate to have dabbled in both industrial properties and office buildings. Now office buildings have a very different type of clientele who go to work every day in these facilities. Almost everyone wears a tie. Industrial clients, by contrast, wear overalls and jeans with work boots and it's usually not a very clean environment. Now that's not a knock on Industrial facilities or companies because they are the backbone of our economy. They make things and distribute them to the country and the world. However, the people working in the two different types of facilities are usually very different. Their dress, etiquette, style, tone, way of communicating and level of professionalism is very different.

I bring this entire story up because of what happens next. One day I'm at my cube, minding my own business, completely immersed in whatever I was into that day and out of the blue, the office administration manager comes to me and says that three senior managers want to see me right away. Now you know that feeling you get when you've just been called into the principal's office and you're not sure what you did but you know it's bad. Well that's exactly what I'm feeling. What the hell did I do? So I sheepishly walk into the room with the kind of body language that says whatever it is I'm sorry and I'll never do it again. Well I immediately notice that they all have big smiles on their faces and a feeling of relief completely baths me but I try not to show it. "So guys what's up?" I say with a little confidence in my voice. "Well Scott as you know you had a great year last tear and we can't thank you enough for your hard work and dedication."

'Ok,' I think, 'this isn't bad so far.' They continue on to say, "We have been thinking as a group that there is a hole in the production team, here in the office, and we'd like to talk to you about it." I think to myself, 'a hole in the production team. What the hell is that?' And they continue on, "Well, land values are on the rise here in South OC, and there is a consistent migration trend of residents because of increased housing starts and that's going to mean a lot more office product being built in the next ten-year cycle."

Don't get me wrong; just because I didn't go to a big school or have a business degree I knew exactly what they were leading to. You see I had made myself read every economic paper on the industry, read every research paper on macro and micro economics, created my own database and written my own newsletter, reporting on the statistics and trends in the market and I knew exactly what these guys were talking about and what they were about to propose. They wanted me to fill the hole in the office team and wanted me to lead the group. I was in, but like every good negotiator wanted to know what was in it for me. Before I even said a word, I calculated the time it would take to retool my business, realign myself with the senior office team, the time it would take to build my brand as the expert in this new specialty and how much of a dip in income I might feel in the short run. I also knew that this was a huge opportunity as our office department was lacking a leader unlike the five super alpha males already vying for supremacy in the industrial division, which I was currently part of.

I responded, "So guys what's in it for me? It sounds daunting!" They go on to say I have their undying support and that I would be receiving my own "Runner." I would be receiving my own "Runner?" You have to understand; getting your own "Runner" is something ten-year vets only rarely receive let alone first year rookies. They went on to say that they would build the department around me and as long as I continued producing I'd continue to receive assistants and "Runner"'s as they graduated and in doing so build my own little force of team mates and with that would come, leverage, free time, extra earners and peace of mind.

So we shake on it and sure enough Carol, a Broker form New Orleans who was looking to migrate to California was my very first

"Runner". Even better, she was a young vet that really only had to be introduced to the market. She had all the instincts of a seasoned vet but just lacked the market knowledge. She has this wonderful infectious laugh that clients love, brains, great instincts and easy on the eyes. We hit it off right away and were an unstoppable force. I made it a point of introducing her to everyone and in short order we dominated the listing market and did more tenant representation business than any other team in our office. We were the go to team when it came time to partner with investment brokers and we made far more money than we set our goals for. Carol graduated from her training program two months early, moved to the Newport Beach office, and went on to make her fortune and we will be lifelong friends.

That year I was among the top five producers in the office again but the staff was getting growing, which meant more competition (although that didn't seem to matter). I just naturally knew I would be among the top five producing brokers in the office and eventually surpass my mentor/trainer (who by the way was just ahead of me and never let me forget it!). The reason I knew this was going to happen was for one reason. I dedicated my professional life to being the best. Not from a place of arrogance, but to prove to myself that I could overcome the odds and be the best. It was my passion.

As the years went on, my teams and I were consistently the go-to guys for our market. I went on to receive a number award several times over the years. I trained many young Runners and always installed the mantra "Be the best." Now my mentor/trainer was occasionally a bit of a tyrant and I had a little of that in me, too, but I always cared deeply for my teammates and protégés as well as co-workers as they were my extended family.

I went on to work for CB Richard Ellis for almost 14 years and those were the best times of my life. During those times and to this date, I've been fortunate to build great relationships with fellow brokers but also with the business leaders in the community. We've shared many great off-work times together. We've been big wave surfing in Fiji, Pipeline on the North shore of Hawaii, and on a 100-foot luxury yacht in Cabo. We've skydived and shark dived is the same day in Hawaii. We've snowboarded from helicopters all over Canada and in the States. We spent ten days with ten guys on a 173-foot Yacht in the Mediterranean, while sightseeing on Capri, Sardinia, San Trope, Majorca, and Ibiza. Without the brokerage business, I would have never had the chance to meet and play with such great people, and for that, I'm eternally thankful for the gifts the business has brought me.

In 2000, with the help of a few buddies we started a company called Enfrastructure and later bought and merged it with a company called TechSpace. We still own and thank the stars we occasionally receive modest checks for our ownership shares even though we no longer have day-to-day operational duties with the company. This company is also a commercial real estate related company so the years in the business paid off here as well.

"TechSpace is the nation's premier full-service facilities and infrastructure provider. We integrate world-class, flexible office space, state-of-the-art technology services, and business process outsourcing solutions, enabling our customers to focus on their core business. In June 2002, California based Enfrastructure acquired New York based TechSpace, a leading provider of alternative office space and infrastructure services to growing and established companies. In June 2003, Enfrastructure formally changed its name to TechSpace to reflect the company's value proposition and leverage the brand awareness built by TechSpace in other markets throughout the years. Today, TechSpace has five locations throughout the United States: Orange County, Los Angeles, and New York (three locations)." www.techspace.com

After helping build TechSpace and making it profitable as Co-founder and EVP of Sales and Marketing, I caught the brokerage bug again and called a couple of my buddies (one of which was an old Runner and Partner by the name of Greg) and we put our team on the market. You have to understand, even though I was out of the market for over three years, fortunately my reputation as a market leader and producer followed me and we shopped ourselves around and found what was the best platform for our clients at the time in a well know company, Grubb & Ellis.

In short order, we became one of the leading teams at Grubb and quickly built back our book of business and continued making the dollars expected in this industry. Eight years at Grubb & Ellis and I was happier than ever although the entrepreneurial bug was in my ear telling me to start my own company. "Give it another shot. Be your own boss. Do it your way"... All the things the bug tells you to do have finally inspired me to go for it. So in the worst economy since the great depression I took the leap to build Bridge Commercial Properties. Fortunately, I have a client base built up over 25 years and the drive of a 20 year old, the wisdom of a 50 year old and a family that inspires me to be the best I can be every day. As a result, I built Bridge Commercial Properties in January 2011.

"Bridge Commercial Properties is a commercial real estate brokerage firm dedicated to its core values, which are providing the highest ethical standards while delivering unsurpassed service and market knowledge, allowing our clients to make better, faster decisions and reducing their overall cost of operations. Bridge Commercial Properties has the combination of a sole proprietor's attention to detail with institutional experience and knowledge. Scott Johnstone, Bridge's founder possess over 25 years of commercial real estate advisory and brokerage experience with a total of over $3B in transactions. Areas of specialty include corporate tenant representation, acquisition and disposition advisory services as well as asset marketing and leasing services in Orange County California. A leader in the industry, Scott Johnstone has managed several brokerage teams representing, everyone from the small mom and pop startup company to public, Technology Entertainment, Financial, Fortune 500 Corporate and government clients. Widely recognized for transaction services locally in Orange County he has also completed numerous complex real estate transactions in major US cities." www.bridgecre.com

I'm very proud of these achievements. They are true stretches for me as compared to where I came from. However, they are not the things that I'm most proud of or bring me the most joy in life. I'm sure, like you, the things that make you happiest in life are family and friends! My children, friends, and grandmother's unconditional love are my core. My greatest calling in life is to pass those gifts onto others. This book is a small attempt to give back the gifts I've received and hopefully help people better their lives.. This is my unconditional love.

It's that love that inspires me and those around me. The knowledge and confidence that someone in my life cared and saw the best in me inspired me to do great things. Now I strive to give people more opportunity and experiences than they ever had as a kid. Such as giving my children the opportunity to shine and become great people with rich lives of their own.

Not only did I do modestly well in business but I also married, had two wonderful kids, and bought a home I never thought possible as a kid. In addition, I made friends with most of the community leaders who are still my friends today. I traveled the world, taught myself to surf, snowboard, and scuba dive. In addition, I taught myself to run a company and to lead and love openly. I pilot my own boat, the third I've owned in partnership with the greatest guy ever, Jimmy U. I have raised my kids to be community leaders. My daughter is a fashion model for the Ford Modeling agency and an honor student. She's poised beyond belief for a 19 year old. She also trains kids how to ride horses and jump English and has her eye on owning her own online fashion company.

My son is a 4.0 student, is 6'2" and won the JV football team MVP award last year. He has a girlfriend who's the sweetest girl in the world and just happens to be a "Volcom" fit model. He surfs, snowboards, spearfishes, and ran Varsity track as a sophomore. Please don't tell him I said this but is one of the calmest and thoughtful young men I have ever met. (Shhh.)

So that's my journey. One filled with strife, overcoming the odds, hard work, faith, and success. It's a story that keeps on going every day but there is one thing I've now dedicated my life to. I'm dedicated to giving anyone (who is willing to listen, learn, and act) the opportunity to do just what I did: build a fulfilling life and do it on your own terms. I was fortunate to have been given a shot. It doesn't matter who you are as long as you want it badly enough. We are living in tough times and it doesn't matter if you're a student, a worker in search of a change, someone in the industry trying to up your game or whomever. In this book, I'm going to give you the step-by-step process, strategically, tactically, psychologically, and with my personal insights to be great in this business.

One thing! This is not a get rich quick program. This is a life changer and anything worth doing is worth doing well. This will take time, but remember that it's all worth it. I'll be here for you as a mentor, all the way, no matter what. So I welcome you to the journey to changing your life, your perspective on wealth and building a better future for yourself and your family.

Chapter Three

The Ten Commandments of the Million-Dollar Broker

There are absolute undying truths for being the type of Broker who consistently produces $1,000,000 in gross commissions or more. They fall into what I call commandments, but they really are life lessons for this business. As I mentioned before, there has been an influx of get rich quick guys in the industry and they rarely know – let alone practice – these commandments. The guy I mentioned in the first chapter practices them unconscientiously every day, as they are part of his character. As much as I'm going to give you lessons on how to be the best broker, I'm also going to give you the lessons I've learned over a 50-year lifetime of how to be the best business person possible.

Now I'm no one to preach and this isn't some religious sermon but there's a hard way to go through life and business and there's an easy way. Now because of my upbringing I've usually chosen the hard way and if I can help you avoid those mistakes this book has done its job. A smart man once asked me why I chose to swim upstream, when the rest of the world is swimming downstream. He said, "It's so much easier to swim with the current!" That is my first bit of advice: swim with the current, just do it intelligently. So here we go. I'm going to give you a brief look at the Ten Commandments and then dedicate a chapter to each. If you need me to elaborate further contact me directly and I will be more than happy to do so.

I.   Choose where and whom to work with wisely.

There are almost an infinite number of firms out there and a hand full of major ones. Do your homework, find an insider/mentor in each of the firms you're thinking about, and get to know them. Take them to lunch. Pick their brain; ask them what's good, bad, or ugly about where they work. Usually, they'll tell you everything, but a manager won't. His interest is somewhat aligned with you because he makes money when you do. However, they are political beings and will only tell you what they want you to hear. So make a broker friend or two within the firm and try to find one of the top producers, as they have the best perspective and knowledge, as they have made it their business. That's why they are where they are, as this is a connection, information, and process business. The broker with the best combination of all three wins. So do your homework in advance and start weighing the options. Picking the right mentor and partners can mean the difference between being good and being great, so take your time, ask around. Everyone has a reputation. Eventually you're going to be your own boss but you might as well just pick up a great partner or two in the process.

The alternative to working for someone else is to build your own company. At least you'll really know who you're working for and you don't split commissions with the house. The benefits are that you answer to yourself and your client's alone. No pecking orders or layers of managers you have to kiss up to. All you have to do is surround yourself with good people, have a good business plan, a good value proposition and a strong differentiator and things should go well. Now that's a simplified version of it but I'll get into the nuts and bolts of it in the next chapter. The downside is that these are tough times. Therefore, you're going to need enough financial runway to last you two years. Now my financial runway came in the way of having built up a client base that follows me pretty much anywhere. That client base combined with my shares in TechSpace (I receive a small but important check bi annually) enabled me to set up my own shop. The worries and fears will be there from time to time as with any job but the rewards of running your own show are indescribable. You'll work twice as has you ever have for at least two years and maybe more depending on the economy, but it's yours and the feeling of pride is worth all the sleepless nights because in the end if you follow the commandments you'll make it and make it big. See my 6-CD series on, "How to Build Your Own Million Dollar Brokerage Firm" www.commercialrealestatebrokersacademy.com

II.   Specialize.

Now there are several choices and you'll have to find what best suits you, and your background, preferences, likes, dislikes, intellect, geographic, personality and desires for your future. Generally, the following are the primary types of property specialists.

1. Office Properties
2. Industrial Properties
3. Retail Properties
4. Land Sales
5. Institutional Investment Sales
6. Private Client Group Investment Sales
7. Multi Family Investment Sales
8. Hotel and Resort Sales

In this chapter focusing on "Specialization," I'll give you as much insight into what I think are the best area's to focus, but ultimately, you'll decide based on a myriad of choices presented to you by your life experiences, connections, and advice from those in your market.

III.   Be the best.

This chapter will cover the most information in the book, as it should. If you're going to commit to this industry, which I know you will, you might as well commit to being the best: the go-to broker. This will be the biggest advantage to you making more money, having better relationships and having the life you always dreamed of. It's not that big of a difference from being good and being the best. It's mainly commitment and some insight on how to do it and that's where I come in. I'll show you the rules of the road the step-by-step process of being the best.

IV.   Drink from the seven buckets of revenue.

There are primarily seven ways to make money in this business. Some specialties have less than others but for my specialty there are seven and that's a good thing because this is a cyclic industry and there are different buckets of revenue that are robust in a down market but some that are not. Make no mistake, all seven buckets of revenue will be available in the good times. However, it's the measure of the broker who can thrive when things are down, so you should know all seven inside and out, in order to have the revenue you want. Keep in mind I'm speaking from the perspective of an "Office Broker." one who specializes in office buildings and land within my market and wants to take advantage of all the buckets of revenue my market offers. In the Chapter on Revenue, I'll go into all the specialties and give relative examples of where they make money but for now, here is how an Office Broker can make money.

1. Exclusively listing property for lease.
2. Exclusively listing income property for sale.
3. Exclusively listing owner occupied property for sale.
4. Exclusive tenant representation for lease.
5. Exclusive user / buyer representation to purchase.
6. Corporate sale lease back.
7. Land sales.

V. Set measurable, personal, business, financial, and life goals and review them quarterly.

I'd like to reference Tony Robbins loosely. There was a study of a large group of similar people, who were asked to do just this. After a period of five years, a study was done on the group. Of the participants in the study, only five percent (5%) followed through and actually practiced this process. They were found to earn more than the entire rest of the study group combined and found to live richer, fuller more involved lives to boot. Need I say more?

VI. Be a person you can be proud of.

Ethics are a personal choice. This is a big money business and a very competitive one at that. There will be times when cutting corners, telling half-truths, puffing, backstabbing, speaking poorly behind someone's back or any number of tempting things will pay you big money in the short run but will ruin your reputation for the future. Reputation is one thing that you can never loose. Be it good, bad or hopefully great has everything to do with ethics and that little voice that speaks to you before any choice you're faced with. With assistance of a well-known document called "Code of the West," you'll get a great lesson on the do's and don'ts and some etiquette lessons of the business. This chapter is probably the most important of them all. If you want a real career and life filled with joy, happiness and the respect of your family, your peers and most importantly yourself follow this chapter as though it's scripture for business. At the end of the day in the initial years, you might do slightly less business, but remember: this is a marathon and not a sprint. The broker with the best reputations always is given more opportunity in the end and eventually this one issue will become a huge multiplier of income. If you're going to make this change in your life, as I know you will, be the best you can be and be a person you can be proud of.

VII.   Build lasting relationships.

One day, 10 years from now, in a meeting taking place without your knowledge, someone who you were nice to, gave some advice to, or happened to hit it off with or did something to change their life for the better, will be in a position to recommend a broker for a very lucrative assignment. They are going to remember what you did and they are going to say, hey, I have the right person, and believe me, they are it! Before you know it and without you even having to pitch the business, you have just made an extra $100,000 that year.

I have a buddy named Scott who owns a few well-known companies, where we both met at the early stages of our careers. I went on to become a pretty good broker and he went on to make into Forbes as one of the top 40 wealthiest people under 40 in America. He and I both hit it off at a time when we both had nothing. I represented him and his father in a small deal for their first office space. I really had to go to bat for them against the owner because I had a feeling about their business. I really liked them and wanted them to catch a break. Now they had no money and the owner says to me, "Ok, I'll do the deal with these guys, but if they go down and I'm left holding the bag, you're going to owe me twice the commissions you'll make on this deal." Without hesitation, I said "yes." That relationship has lasted 25 years, and the stories of that friendship could fill several books.

VIII.   It's a marathon, not a sprint.

If this is your get rich quick solution then stop reading now. I mean it. This is a life changer, a career changer, a perspective and wealth changer, but it's not quick. Now I will say that the time will fly by like no other industry you've been in. Remember you get out what you put in so you're going to find that you'll be putting your all into this and when that happens, time flies (but in a good way). First, you'll be a trainee, then a Rookie, then a midlevel vet, and finally the go to broker. It will all happen like a blur, because life is short and you hear that adage often, so take my advice and treat it like a Marathon. If you take your time, prepare properly, and learn as you go, you'll win the race. I have a "Type A" personality and am very impatient by nature, yet sometimes this is a "hurry up and wait" type of business. The sprinters in this business burn out quickly, take short cuts, and hurt their reputations and their families. They are perceived to be in it for the short run and that's not what it's all about. Another adage would be: "It's a chess match not checkers." Think 10 steps ahead not two. I'll go into this more in the chapter to come.

IX.   Have fun while saving money and have a great life!

You're going to make more money than you've ever thought you would. It's a fact. It's going to happen. With this influx in income comes the desire to spend it like it's a constant! Now over time and on average this will be true but until you've established yourself and have a full pipeline on a consistent basis, do yourself the favor of learning the basics of saving and investing. Even after you're the master of the universe, never stop investing because there may come a day when you may want to sail the world for a year, build your own business, open a surf camp and hotel in Costa Rica, or whatever. Most likely, you'll drive the car of your dreams, live in the best neighborhood, have a boat, etc. The thing of it is that you can have all of those things and at the same time peace of mind that if, God forbid, some disaster comes your way, you'll be prepared financially. This is an all commission business and there are cycles both good and bad. And even though you realize this (and your nervous system will learn to take it in stride), you may have a wife who will drive you crazy unless she can see six zero's or more in you financial statement at any given time. I'll also discuss the ultimate killer in life: retirement. Please never do it, but if you do, do it in style. We'll get into the various ways to live the good life while putting enough away to continue to do so if you, for some strange reason, decide to leave the business.

X.   Give back

Now this may seem cliché but the best feeling in the world is giving back to those less fortunate. I believe that charity begins at home so take care of the spouse and kids first. But don't wait too long after being in the business to choose an organization or organizations that you can give your time to, not just money but your time. Volunteer to be on a fundraising committee. Become a Big Brother or Sister or prepare food on a regular basis for the homeless. Volunteer at your local church. Become a board member of one of the local chapters of a major charitable organization. You'll benefit from the knowledge that you're making a difference in people's lives. It's why I'm writing this book. I want those who never had the chance or the support to know there is an alternative and I'm going to give you a leg up. One person did that for me and I want to be that person for as many people that I can reach. The secondary result is that giving to others has a mysterious way of giving back to you. Someone recognizes your work and recommends you for a job. You receive a community award that inspires your kids or someone close to you to do the same. It's the notion of the movie "Pay it forward." Good begets good and who knows before you know it you've made an impact on this world for the better and that's what I believe to be all of our higher callings in life.

Now this is the point in the book where you start to question yourself.

Q: Can I really do this?
A: Absolutely. If you want it bad enough it's yours.

Q: Do I need a special license?
A: No, just a regular real estate license.

Q: Will I be accepted?
A: Be nice, carry yourself with confidence and people will accept you.

Q: Do I have the time?
A: Make the time!

Q: Do I have a mentor?
A: Yes. I'm your first of many to come. People love to help others.

Q: Is this a big change?
A: Not any bigger than changing a job. It's big but that feeling passes.

Q: Do I have what it takes?
A: If you have the desire, a high school degree, and can learn, then YES!

Q: Will my family support me?
A: If you have one, they better, or they'll be left behind and calling for a loan when you make it big.

Q: Will I have the cash until the revenue comes in?
A: Find a way! Live cheap, get roommates, and call in all your markers.

Q: Do I have to wear a suit?

A: Yes. Until you're the Alpha. Then you can wear anything you want.

Q: Will I have to get a new car?
A: You'll have to tour clients and it depends on how big of a shit box you currently have. If you need to, lease something cheap with four doors because in short order you'll have the car you really want.

Q: Can I compete?
A: The competition is internal. Never forget that.

Q: Can I get a job with one of the best firms?
A: If they are hiring and if you follow my steps for interviewing, it will be hard not to want to hire you.

Q: Can I find the right trainer?
A: You already have one in me, so just focus on finding a good one wherever you land.

Q: What will I need if I start my own company?
A:
- Your real estate license in your state,
- articles of incorporation with a fictitious business name, (preferably an S Corp. use an attorney about $1,200),
- a bank account to receive and write checks,
- a phone, a desk, a computer, internet access
- business cards ($50 online),
- a web address and e-mail, (Use Go Daddy. $50 per month)
- Costar Real Estate Information services, $215 per month.
- A website (there are hundreds of premade sites you can customize and they are free if you pay the monthly $50 hosting fee.) There are plenty of books that will walk you through the process. It's not brain surgery. It's basic blocking and tackling.

Q: What are the steps to getting my own company going and getting results?

A: See   www.CommercialRealEstateBrokersAcademy.com   and get my 6 - CD Series, "How to Build Your Own Million Dollar Brokerage Firm"

Q: How long will it take?
A: It will take about twelve to eighteen months to make real money on average depending how hard you work and what your dedication level is.

Q: What technology will I need?
A: A computer. Most firms supply the rest.

Q: Do I need employees?
A: Not if you're with a firm. They have all it takes.

Q: What documentation do I need?
A: A driver's license, auto insurance and a Real Estate License in your state.

Q: How do I get clients?
A: Keep reading, there are several ways and later, I'll go into great detail. Friends, relationships, cold calling and walking buildings introducing you and your services to the tenants and owners for a start.

Q: I can't do this.
A: Once I asked a psychologist buddy of mine about this question. What you're really saying is you don't want to do this because you're afraid of failure. The answer is if you want it enough, you'll *will* yourself to do it. You'll find the courage to say *"What the hell am I waiting for?"* If your reason for change is big enough, you can do anything. This is simply making a job change or choice that takes a little sales skill, organizational skill, making new connections, and a learning a few new processes. If you can mix in some charisma and a little fifth grade math, this is unquestionably "do-able.". Can you do this? Of course you can.

Let me tell you that I asked myself each and every one of these questions repeatedly prior to taking the plunge. This is the natural process of gauging risk versus reward. We have two basic forces driving us. They are *fear* and *greed*. Fear is always the dominant emotion, as it's a survival instinct. We have all heard of "fight or flight response" Flight is the fear part and fight is the greed part of this equation. I don't know where you are in your life, so I can't answer these questions for you. But I do know this. This opportunity is worth fighting for.

I also know this. I came from the wrong side of the tracks. I had very little family support - my depression era grandmother was the only one behind me emotionally. I had very little financial resources when I made the plunge to learn this business; I was a retail sales. employee making maximum $35,000 per year with not much future ahead of me. I hadn't graduated college but I did have a few things going for me. Number one was courage, I knew I had it in me and knew if given the opportunity I could do anything.

Second, I had a mentor and I'm here to tell you that if you'll have me then I'm honored to walk you through the process and be your mentor, plus I'll help you find others who will advocate you.

The third thing I had was desire. I had that hunger - that thing that drives you to prove to yourself that you can be better. It's hard to describe "it" but if you have "it," you know it. That one thing is all it takes. The rest will take care of itself. Have faith in yourself. Tell people about your desire to succeed and they will naturally get behind you. The best quality in people is that they naturally like to help others. Build your courage, fuel your desire, build your team and I'll help you accomplish the rest.

Chapter Four

Commandment I: Choose Where and Whom to Work with Wisely

Commercial property exists to serve the residential base that surrounds it. Other contributing factors to the size of the Commercial Real Estate base in a given area are the number of shipping ports, commercial and international airports, railroads, freeway systems, free trade zones, residential development, and a positive population migration trend.

The statistical data for major cities charting migration, population growth, unemployment, available base of commercial property is constantly changing. Go to these websites to do your research on the best market for you.

- US Census Bureau www.census.gov
- www.cbre.com (market research section)
- www.cushwake.com (market research section)
- www.grubb-ellis.com (market research section)

If your current city isn't on the Census.gov list, don't worry, neither is mine. I'm in Orange County, California and we have a base of office space that is approximately 100,000,000 square feet. There are hundreds of markets around the United States that have commercial bases of product that will support hundreds of brokers, that the best of which will make a million dollars a year or more. I focus on a relatively small patch of office property of approximately 35,000,000 square feet and in my early years, which were some of my best, my base of product to work on was a mere 5,000,000 square feet. Income is determined by how much market share you have, buildings you list, tenants you represent, buildings you sell, land you sell for development etc. It's ok to be a big fish in a small pond or vice versus, just do your homework and find a market your comfortable living near and choose it. It's probably in your own back yard.

Go to www.BridgeCommercialProperties.com/realreport to view the latest version of our newsletter and understand the measurable metrics in my market.

The next step is to research all the major commercial brokerage firms in your area or the area you want to focus on. Next, call them all and ask for the manager. After leaving a few voicemails regarding how much you would like to come work for the firm, your call will eventually be returned. When your call is returned your sole goal is to get a recommendation and contact information for a top broker in the office who you can speak to about the business. You can also do this online, as every firm lists their brokers and managers. You want to make an impression that you have desire, are tenacious, and you want the manager to remember your name as well as refer you to the broker himself. So be persistent and apologize for being a pest but be exactly that because tenacity is what he's looking for. Below is a list of the top firms I've surveyed but results change based on the market you're in, so do your research. Also, it's the person you work for as much as the company so choose well.

CB Richard Ellis is the global leader in real estate services. Each year, they complete thousands of successful assignments with clients from the gamut of industries. This volume creates market knowledge that allows them to seize opportunities, speed the business process and creates the most thorough, precisely accurate picture of global commercial real estate conditions and trends. Every day, in markets around the globe, they apply their insight, experience, intelligence, and resources to help clients make informed real estate decisions.

Colliers International provides a range of services to commercial real estate users, owners, investors and developers worldwide. Primary services include consulting, corporate solutions, investment services, landlord and tenant representation, project management, property and asset management, valuation and advisory services. The organization serves the hotel, industrial, mixed-use, office, retail, and residential property sectors.

Jones Lang LaSalle is a financial and professional services firm specializing in real estate services and investment management. Their more than 30,000 people in 750 locations in 60 countries serve the local, regional, and global real estate needs of those clients, growing the company in the process. In response to changing client expectations and market conditions, they assemble teams of experts who deliver integrated services built on market insight and foresight, sound research and relevant market knowledge.

Cushman & Wakefield assists clients in every stage of the real estate process, representing them in the buying, selling, financing, leasing, managing, and valuing of assets, as well as providing strategic planning and research, portfolio analysis, site selection and space location, among many other advisory services. Its 13,000 worldwide employees, located in 231 offices throughout 58 countries, assess each client's needs and implement solutions that fit the client's strategic, operational, and financial goals.

Grubb & Ellis Company is one of the largest commercial real estate services and investment companies in the world. With 6,000 professionals in more than 100 company owned and affiliate offices, Grubb & Ellis Company draws from a unique platform of real estate services, practice groups and investment products to deliver comprehensive, integrated solutions to real estate owners, tenants and investors. The firm's transaction, management, consulting, and investment services are supported by highly regarded proprietary market research and extensive local expertise.

Coldwell Banker Commercial With a collaborative network of independently owned and operated affiliates, the organization comprises over 220 companies and more than 3,400 professionals throughout the U.S., as well as internationally. In fact, CBC possesses the largest geographic footprint in today's commercial real estate marketplace. The organization's worldwide headquarters are in Parsippany, NJ.

NAI Global professionals provide a full spectrum of services available to regional, national, and international clients via its global network of independent commercial real estate brokerage companies. Clients will have a primary point of contact, who will leverage all of NAI's enterprise resources wherever they need them around the world. In addition, the company's leading edge technology will support all their global moves, from streamlining a business unit, to extracting value from the client's portfolio, to more efficient management of their projects and leases worldwide.

Cassidy Turley has advocated for clients for more than 100 years. The firm has 430 million square feet of managed space, 60 offices, 23 national markets, and more than $17 billion in completed transactions for 2010. The company is also a dominant provider of Capital Markets and Corporate Services—serving more than 25,000 locations.

Cresa Partners, since the founding of the firm, the primary focus of has been to serve the best interests of tenants. By representing tenants, not landlords, they strive to ensure objectivity and avoid conflicts of interest. Unlike traditional real estate firms, they are service oriented, not transaction oriented. They provide an array of integrated corporate services and work to align its client's real estate needs with their business plans. Cresa advisors and project managers form partnerships with their clients, providing ongoing service that goes "beyond the deal."

The Sperry Van Ness organization of affiliates is the only brokerage firm that markets all properties on a national basis to a 100,000strong brokerage and investment community. Because of its national reach that includes primary, secondary and tertiary markets, the Sperry Van Ness Organization excels at seamlessly locating investment options on behalf of clients across the country while leveraging the power of all brokers — even those with competing firms.

TCN Worldwide is continuously improving its services and processes by anticipating the needs of members and their clients and utilizing the years of local expertise of the members. At the same time, they are constantly developing and implementing the future innovations, which will ensure the company's long-term success and position the member firms as leaders within their local market.

CORFAC International is an organization of independently owned commercial real estate services firms with local and regional expertise throughout the Americas, Europe, and Asia. CORFAC firms specialize in office, R&D and industrial brokerage, corporate real estate services, investment property sales, tenant representation, land sales, retail leasing, property management and property consulting.

Newmark in January of 2006 formed a partnership with London based **Knight Frank**, forming **Newmark Knight Frank**, a global real estate consultancy with extensive worldwide capabilities and coverage throughout North America, Europe, Asia Pacific, Latin America, Africa and the Middle East. The Newmark Knight Frank partnership now operates more than 220 offices in established and emerging property markets on six continents. With a staff of 7,300 employees, they have created an effective global platform from which to serve the property needs of their growing list of clients.

Marcus & Millichap Real Estate Investment Services, since 1971, has been the premier provider of investment real estate brokerage services. The foundation of its investment sales is the depth of their local market knowledge. Their 40year history of maintaining investor relationships in local markets enables them to be the best information source and transaction service provider nationally.

Duke Realty has been a leader in commercial real estate development since its founding in 1972 in Indianapolis, Indiana,. From its first property—Building One in Park 100 Business Park on the northwest side of Indianapolis—Duke Realty has set the standard for providing high-quality, innovative, and distinctive environments that meet businesses' operating needs.

King Sturge is one of the largest international property consultancies with a network of over 210 wholly owned, associated, and affiliated offices in 45 countries worldwide. In Europe, they operate in the major UK commercial centers and principal mainland European cities. In the Americas, King Sturge has business partners in North, Central, and South America through King Sturge CORFAC International and Chain Links Retail Advisors.

Lee & Associates' last year's group of companies successfully completed transactions with a total value of nearly $7 billion. Not only has Bill Lee's profit-sharing concept proven enormously successful, but also it has fueled the explosive growth of group offices throughout the West and now moving east.

DTZ Barnicke, headquartered in Toronto, has 19 full service offices across Canada with an excess of 500 employees. DTZ Barnicke acts as a broker to service tenants, landlords, developers, owners, investors, governments and institutions locally, nationally and internationally.

ONCOR International is a premier global commercial real estate system, whose members include over 50 independent brokerages with over 170 offices in 32 countries. Collectively the members have been responsible for approximately $13.2 billion in commercial real estate volume in 2009.

Prudential Commercial real estate is the commercial real estate division of Prudential Real Estate and Relocation Services, Inc., an integrated real estate brokerage franchise and relocation services business. Their professionals are committed with integrity and professionalism.

Studley's success is derived from its rich history, coupled with its ongoing innovation and cutting-edge ideas. The company has always valued individual merit but also understands that the aggregate of those individuals provides a result far more powerful. It's a culture founded on trusting relationships.

Excerpts of this report were borrowed from Commercial Trainer, Mike Lipsey

The next and most important step is to present yourself as a commodity to each of the finalist firms you choose to interview with because that should be your attitude. You're going to be making them money. You need to choose wisely and what they have to offer will be the determining factor. Do this with grace and a humble tone but remember you want to work for the right guy and the right company. So here are two sets of checklists to picking both.

Brokerage Company Requirements:

- A brand that is respected for their ethics and caliber of brokers.

- Management teams who are proactive in the market and can help bring in business.

- A network of brokers who you can give and receive referrals from multiple markets other than your own.

- A property management wing of the company that you can refer business to and receive referrals from.

- Multiple specialists in the office that you can refer business to and can receive referrals from in return.

- An investment team that is known for being one of the best. Without this, you and your team will never realize a large portion of this type of revenue.

- A friendly and cooperative group of specialists within your specialty who you'll enjoy going to battle with every day and can see yourself collaborating with.

- An administrative staff that is competent, caring and cooperative.

- An administrative manager who actually likes brokers and is open, friendly, good to the staff and therefore maintains high moral. Furthermore, this manager's first word cannot be "No" when you ask for a budget expenditure on behalf of a client.

- A research department that cares about excellence and goes the extra mile for you because the best information can often make or break a deal.

- A company's bottom line should be healthy and not in the news constantly for speculation that they may headed for bankruptcy or sale.

- A healthy budget to spend on client needs, signs, brochures, websites, mailers, open houses, presentation materials etc.

- You don't want to work in a shark tank, or with an office that has a few bad apples because they will make work miserable so ask the hard questions and choose wisely.

Mentor/Broker Trainer requirements:

- They should have done this before and been through the experience of training a new salesperson.

- Their previous Runners/Trainees should say good things about them.

- They should have enough variety and volume of business to keep you constantly busy and show you all the aspects of your chosen specialty.

- They should treat you with respect. A good amount of friendly hazing is to be expected but there is a difference between friendly and mean spirited riding.

- They should have a general business plan written for you for the year or two you'll be there so you know what to expect and what is expected of you.

- They should share their business plan and goals so you can be as effective in attaining those goals as soon as possible.

- You and your team should have monthly review meetings that include prospects, deal flow, responsibilities, and revenue review. In addition, the meetings should include actual versus goal income year to date, prospective client hit lists and responsibilities as well as progress reports.

- They should be an ethical and honor driven person. There's nothing worse than getting a bad reputation for working for the wrong person before you've had a chance to prove yourself on your own.

- They should be a good person and someone you can respect and get along with because you want to be motivated every day by the job at hand and not have to worry about the temperament of your mentor.

- They should have a good work ethic and organizational skills and killer presentation skills. This is a huge game changer. It's your job getting him in the room with the client; it's his job to close the client. Killer presentation skills and instinct is right up there with the top attributes.

- Salesmanship. This job is a sales position and you should never forget it. Your mentor should be able to teach you the finer points and you should always be learning the basics on your own.

Chapter Five

Commandment II: Specialize

I previously touched on the various fields of specialty within the Commercial Brokerage world. In this chapter, we will discuss how you'll choose your eventual specialty and what to expect from each. You'll choose your field of specialty based on many factors. It may be as simple as it's the only job available to you and so there you go. Hopefully, you'll do a little research to match your choice with your innate skill sets and proclivity to the industry sector. You should do this while gauging your potential success based on market size, mentor, and company strength in the chosen fields of specialty.

Once again the fields are as follows:

1. Office Properties
2. Industrial Properties
3. Retail Properties
4. Land Sales
5. Investment Properties, Institutional and Private Client Group
6. Multi Family Investment Sales
7. Hotel & Resort Sales

I'll take a moment to explain each and give you enough knowledge to ask the right questions of your potential manager, mentor, and interviewers as well as to get a feeling for what your calling might be.

1. Office properties: Typically built in urban and suburban areas, these buildings are built for specific corporations to lease or own as their corporate headquarters. More often than not they're built by a merchant developer. This person perceives a need for the building in the market based on supply and demand then purchases a parcel of land and build's the building caliber to meet the needs of the consumer base in the area which are mostly companies who have a client/employee base in that area. More often than not, the projects are multi-tenant buildings that are divided into various sizes to accommodate prospective tenants with the hope of leasing the building to 100% occupancy so to maximize the owner's profits. Make no mistake these are income producing properties that in the big scheme of international finance are a hedge against inflation and a source of solid, continuous income because they are tangible assets, not just stock or a piece of paper. These buildings cater to white-collar workers who are trying to present an image to their customers and shareholders while also building their brands.

Often, you'll see the name of a major corporation on a sign atop an office building. You may think they're the sole tenant in the building and 90% of the time you'd be wrong, as signage usually goes to the biggest, most prestigious tenant with the best credit. This is typically as much a major point of negotiation as it is a big branding advantage to the tenant, and a big marketing advantage to the landlord.

Office real estate needs span a variety of aspects from small companies to national and international requirements. Office professionals should collaborate as experts in their primary markets, knowing all aspects of owners and tenants needs. Typical office professionals have available to them property databases and reporting tools, combined with research and extensive market knowledge to advise their clients to make a myriad of decisions that allow them to gain maximum profit while mitigating losses.

Landlord representation
Asset analysis
Competition analysis
Development of prospect profile
Comparable transactions
Development of pricing strategy
Full-service property marketing
Land analysis and sales
Lease proposal negotiations
Lease negotiations
In-depth Market analysis

Tenant/ Owner occupier representation
Property analysis
Renewal strategy
Comparative analysis
Situation analysis
Option development
Project implementation
Own vs. lease analysis
Lease versus lease comparison and cost analysis
Negotiation strategies
Occupancy cost reduction program

2. Industrial properties: Industrial Services is one of the largest brokerage service lines in the world. Industrial professionals have a deep understanding of current and emerging technologies, production processes, and global business practices. A well-trained industrial broker should be able to meet the precise space utilization needs of their clients for manufacturing, assembly, research and development, distribution, and warehouse facilities and land assignments.

Highly skilled Industrial Brokers should have a proven track record in successfully marketing client properties for sale, lease or sublease and should also be particularly well versed at representing companies in relocations and/or expansions. They also should offer consulting on land planning, infrastructure design, and marketing of speculative buildings and should be skilled at arranging build- to-suits for industrial facilities, providing site selection options, and handling land acquisitions/dispositions.

Industrial Services should align client business strategies with customized real estate solutions under local market conditions. Supported by up-to-date knowledge of local, regional, and national industrial markets, the broker should match the financial, operational, and qualitative needs of clients with appropriate real estate opportunities.

Industrial tenant representation:
Current situation and business plan analysis
Build-to-suit transaction services

Expert advice on land use provisions
Access local and regional market data for comparative studies
Lease versus buy analysis
Land acquisitions
Comprehensive property availability studies
Situation analysis
In-depth market summaries
Proposal negotiations
Lease negotiations
Negotiation Strategies and tactics

Industrial landlord representation:
Sale/lease of existing facilities
Sale/leaseback transactions
Valuation studies
Land acquisitions
Property valuations
Consulting services
Asset Marketing

3. Retail properties: The retail Broker's goal is simple. It's to partner with clients to understand business objectives and create innovative ways to optimize the value of real estate assets. Retailing is much more than "space" or a "place to do business." Retail real estate is an environment. And while the business drivers behind a retail real estate decision may be somewhat predictable, the physical and psychological forces that conspire to create the ideal environment for each client vary significantly. Understanding these variations, no matter how subtle, is an important component of the value a good broker brings. It's what allows you to help your clients make the right decision.

Retail tenant representation: Every retailer is unique. Whether the people the retail broker serves have one location or one thousand, whether their interest is acquisition or disposition, you should have solutions to meet their individual needs.

Retail experts should be ready and able to offer their clients insight into the latest market trends. Good research tools, including a competitive analyses, demographic studies, and tenant mix comparisons are an invaluable part of your clients' decision-making processes. It's this kind of knowledge that makes you much more than agents or brokers; you're your clients' business partners.

Typical services you should provide as a retail tenant representation broker are:
Key Market Identification
Store Placement Strategy
Site Selection
Competitive Analysis
Mapping & Demographic Tools
Tenant Mix Synergy
Trade Area Trends
Consumer Profiling
Market Potential Reports
Deal Validation
Warehousing and Distribution Services
Demographic Reports
Situation Analysis
In-depth Market Summaries
Proposal Negotiations
Lease Negotiations
Negotiation Strategies and Tactics

Retail landlord representation: Retail property owners need and deserve a personalized approach delivered by professionals who partner with our ownership clients to maximize value by leveraging the capital they have invested - whether it's a single market asset or a multi-market portfolio.

We serve developers, institutions, and private investors with the following service offerings:
Brokerage Services, Sales & Leasing
Development Advisory
Asset Services
Investment Sales
Capital Markets

Valuation & Advisory Services
Consumer Marketing
Research & Consulting
Property Marketing Strategies and Tactics

The areas of specialty retail brokers typically cover are:
Anchor Retailers
Entertainment
Food & Drug
Lifestyle
Malls
Mixed-Use Properties
Neighborhood Centers
Restaurants
Urban Retail

4. Land owner services: Land Services provides landowners with the comprehensive ability to evaluate the highest and best use of a particular land property. You become an expert on land entitlement and offer your extensive knowledge of local market conditions, competitive land parcels and the regulatory environment, to assist landowners in formulating a strategy for maximizing the value of their real estate holdings. I highly recommend you assemble a collaborative team of specialists in retail, office, or industrial properties to market and sell land parcels directly to end users and developers, and maximize the market presence of listed properties through a robust database of qualified buyers and developers, as well as the brokerage community.

Land investor and developer services: Land Services bring together local market knowledge, serving the property needs of investors and developers, and providing a competitive advantage by capitalizing on market conditions. Build a group of professional friends that are tightly integrated across service lines that will be you're go-to team when you have the right land buyer deal no matter what the zoning or use requirements.

5. Investment properties, institutional and private client group: Investment Property Services provide customized, asset-appropriate investment sales, acquisition and recapitalization specialized by client type, geographic coverage and property sector.

Investment Property Services is segmented into two separate but integrated and complementary groups: **The Institutional Group** responds to the sophisticated needs of institutional clients, while **The Private Client Group** serves the unique needs of private and individual property investors. Both groups differ in focus, yet are identical in their dedication to client service. By integrating market research with online investor databases such as "Real Capital Markets," Investment Property Brokers analyze market cycles, anticipate trends and command capital in local regional and national markets. Investment Property clients include domestic and foreign-based individuals and institutional real estate investors, opportunity funds, owner/developers, REITs and entities with tax-sensitive exit strategies. Investment brokers are best to collaborate with local market-leading professionals specializing in office, industrial, retail, multi-housing and hotels, as well as numerous niche specialty practice brokers to maximize their sales and therefore income.

6. Multi-family investments: Apartment sales

Investor interest in U.S. multi-family properties continued at a healthy clip at the beginning of 2011, as investment sales dollar volume jumped 40% in the first quarter over the same period last year. More deals closed than in any quarter since mid-2005, according to CoStar Group data.

Just fewer than 4,000 multifamily sales transactions were recorded in the quarter at a total volume of $9.4 billion, according to preliminary CoStar sales data, compared with $6.7 billion in first-quarter 2010 and just $3.76 billion in first-quarter 2009. Despite the heightened activity, sales were just 22% of their mid- 2007 market peak of $43 billion in the most recent quarter. Sales volumes declined about $6 billion from fourth-quarter 2010. While leasing fundamentals are no longer improving at last year's torrid pace, investor interest by all accounts remained sharp for quality apartment product. Renter demand for apartment units remained solid in the first quarter, as the supply of new units continued to dwindle and the national apartment vacancy rate fell to 7.4%, a decline of 100 basis points since late 2009.

Despite an uneven economic expansion, "fundamentally, the outlook for the economy remains one of recovery and growth, and CoStar remains optimistic about its prospects. That is good news for Commercial real estate and good news for apartment demand," said CoStar Real Estate Strategist Kevin White during the Washington, D.C.-based company's recent First Quarter 2011 Multifamily Review & Outlook.

Investor appetite for newer institutional-grade product in high- barrier coastal markets is driving sales volume in recent quarters, unlike 2008 and 2009, when larger transactions were difficult to finance and the limited pool of mostly local investors opted for smaller properties in suburban locations, explained CoStar Senior Real Estate Strategist Michael Cohen, who co-presented the outlook with White.

REITs and private equity firms were the dominant net buyers of multifamily property in the first quarter. REITs purchased a total of $515 million in the quarter, with $130 million in net purchases after subtracting dispositions. Private equity player netted $117 million in sales, an amount expected rise into 2012. Institutions were the largest apartment sellers, disposing of a net $354 million in assets.

Washington, D.C. and Los Angeles logged the highest year- to-date sales volume at $900 million, followed by the San Francisco Bay Area ($600 million), Phoenix ($500 million), and Long Island ($400 million). The top five multifamily markets accounted for $3.3 billion, about 35% of the $9.4 billion in total sales volume. Collectively, those top markets saw a 15% year- over-year increase in the first quarter. "Core investors are still very interested in paying up for stability and low volatility," Cohen said. "Pricing has been strong in D.C., but it still took the top spot for multifamily investment dollars."

The distressed transactions market, including REO sales, deeds in lieu of foreclosure and properties with high vacancy and/or deferred maintenance costs, accounted for about 21% of all multifamily sales volume in the first quarter. While still quite high, the percentage of distressed deals declined 5% from the previous quarter, however, and CoStar expects distress levels to slowly drift down as fundamentals continue to improve.

In housing exposed markets like Tucson, Fresno, Jacksonville, Las Vegas, and Atlanta, distressed trades exceeded 60% of all transactions. Supply constrained markets like Boston, Marin/Sonoma counties, CA, San Diego, northern New Jersey, Portland, Washington, D.C., and San Jose, showed distressed levels of 20% or less.

OCCUPANCY, RENTS RISE EVEN AS ABSORPTION SLOWS

While the drop in the homeownership rate has led to higher absorption of apartments over the last five quarters, the pace has slowed from last year's 167,000 units absorbed, which was the strongest level of demand since 2005. The last two quarters have seen demand of 19,000 and 23,000 units, respectively.

CoStar forecasts total supply additions of just 27,000 units in the 54 largest markets in 2011, just one-third of the pre-recession average between 2003 and 2008. However, CoStar expects to see occupancy gains in 49 out of the 54 metros over the next three quarters, led by San Antonio, Houston, Raleigh, Salt Lake City, Orlando, and Portland. Markets such as Richmond, Norfolk, Seattle, Cincinnati, and St. Louis will see modest increases in vacancy.

The limited supply of Class A and B properties continues to generate the most demand, resulting in fewer rent concessions a strong effective rent growth in 2011.

Three of the five top markets for rent growth in 2011 are in the supply constrained San Francisco Bay Area, led San Francisco (7.3%), and San Jose (7%). The East Bay, Honolulu and Boston round out the top five, followed closely by Phoenix, Raleigh, Washington, Baltimore and Denver.

As published by Costar's May 18 2011, Multi family report. http://www.costar.com/News/Article/Multifamily-Investment-Leasing-Fundamentals-Off-to-Solid-Start-In-2011/1288

7. Hotel & resort investment group:

Your Group should understand the unique challenges and opportunities that come with investing in and divesting hotel properties. Professionals who choose to specialize in this sector and devote their careers to following the properties, investors, and owners that trade in this space. You should know the hotel market inside and out and strive to build client relationships that endure. Your Hotel group's mission is to be the single strategic advisor to your clients for the provision of lodging real estate services focused on the acquisition and disposition of hotels, resorts, gaming, and golf and leisure properties worldwide.

The areas of specialty hotel investment groups typically cover are:
Hotel Capital Markets
Sales
Investment Advisory
Valuation
Development
Asset Management
Global Gaming
Golf and Resort Properties
Leisure and Alternative Investment
Pubs
Operator Selection

If your team is specifically dedicated to luxury, gaming, golf and resort properties, your hotel group has the ability to bring specialized knowledge and experience to each and every deal, regardless of the client's needs. Your specific Hotel Group should be comprised of a highly qualified team of professionals whose mission is to focus on the specific needs of their respective sectors within the lodging industry. These brokers' mission includes the acquisition and disposition of properties, raw land zoned for development, appraisals, project consulting, property and facilities management, and financial services. Being successful in this highly specialized and volatile marketplace demands a dedicated, professional approach. Combining your talents and experience, you'll bring a unique perspective to the brokerage and appraisal of all hospitality real estate.

From a single asset in a local market, to a sophisticated portfolio across multiple locations, each assignment benefits from your market-making ability. Your synchronized approach to marketing brings your owner clients to the market – and your buyer clients to the opportunity – with unprecedented speed and efficiency. You anticipate trends, seize opportunities, and leverage your network to help your clients realize their investment goals.

In order to efficiently manage the marketing process and ensure optimal exposure of an investment opportunity, you'll have to implement a shared platform that manages investor criteria as well as client and market information. Information should be updated daily on a real-time basis to keep pace with the ever-changing environment. This platform increases speed to market by allowing your teams to launch a comprehensive marketing campaign in a short period of time. By leveraging a combination of cutting edge technology and industry savvy team members, you're effectively putting the collective knowledge of the entire group to work for your clients.

Chapter Six:

Commandment III: Be the Best!

The Many Sides of Success

If you want a thing bad enough
To go out and fight for it
Work day and night for it,
Give up your time and your peace and your sleep for it,
If only desire of it
Makes you hold all other things tawdry and cheap for it,
If life seems all empty and useless without it,
And all that you scheme and you dream is about it,
If gladly you'll sweat for it,
Fret for it, Plan for it,
Lose all your terror of God or man for it,
If you'll simply go after that thing that you want,
With all your capacity,
Strength and sagacity,
Faith, hope, confidence, stern pertinacity,
If neither cold poverty,
Famished and gaunt,
Nor sickness nor pain
Of body or brain
Can turn you away from the thing that you want,
You'll Get it!!!

Berton Braley

Now Berton Braley is one of our most optimistic American poets and this is one of my favorites. His critics might say, why give up life for one thing. The thing I'm hoping you become is the best in your market in your selected specialty and not to the exclusion of all else although the poem may suggest that. If I had to put into words the feeling and desire I had as I began my career these would have been them. In retrospect I would add a bit more about the wisdom of balance, but in the beginning and until you're up and running, this is your mantra. Read it daily!

This is the most important commandment of all. As someone once said, "Shoot for the stars and you'll at least hit the moon." Well, my motto is: *Go big or go home.* So let's go big. Rome was not built in a day and neither will your empire but there are some basics to being great and this chapter will cover them.

First, you must adopt the mindset that you'll be the best in something before you can actually do it. I don't care where the drive comes from but it should be from a place of good and the desire to be great. Think big and achieve it. For me it came from a place where I felt inferior because of my lack of pedigree so I was going to prove that I was the best no matter what it took. As I said I usually learn the hard way. Please take my advice to find a way of combining that burning desire to win at all costs with a win/win mentality and you'll be great.

Let's cover some basic ground, strategies and tactics, as well as start thinking and building on the practices of "The Greats" that have gone before you. These are not secrets but tried and true methods for being great.

1. **Write a business plan:** Where do you want to focus your time? What specialty or niche within the market will you choose? What do you want to be? Create a mission statement, organizational chart, value proposition, and set out differentiators that set you apart from the competition. Set specific goals both functional and financial.

2. **Define team roles:** Define your team role and also team members' roles if you are on a team. If you are not on a team, I highly suggest being part of one. Team Leader/Rainmaker, cold caller, document processor, marketing coordinator/administrative assistant, "Runner", or sometimes-financial analyst. Everyone has his or her own likes and skill sets. Try to align those skill sets and workload accordingly, as this will leverage the time of the team and make you all more money

and more consistent money without the swings in income a lone soldier can experience. If you have the personality and the ability to cold call and bring in business, then the highest paid member on a team will eventually be you. Or you'll eventually be the team leader.

3. **Be a leader through example and people will naturally want to follow you:** This is most important when it comes to your clients. Your clients have hired you to lead them so that is exactly what you will do. If you truly are a leader, everyone in the room will naturally perceive it through your body language, demeanor, and tone. One little phrase will work wonders in having clients, partners and employees follow your ideas: "May I make a suggestion?" People will naturally say "Yes!" You better have a full plan of attack, strategies, tactics, materials, and roles already thought out for what you're trying to achieve and it better work. If you can pull that off, you're a natural leader and you better earn it through example every day because the benefits will be incredible.

4. **Work ethic:** Be in the office first and out last -, at least for the first year and the impression you make will last a lifetime. Additionally, you'll be creating work habits that the best of the best adhere to and will follow you through your career. You'll accomplish twice as much as anyone else and if you follow my guidance you will be working smart as well and your income will be reflective of both hard and smart work.

5. **Ethics:** They have to be at your core, no matter what, and forever. You have to always tell the blunt truth, even if you messed up. You can't leave out even the smallest omission or detail or nuance to a conversation or situation. Don't puff to make you sound better or as though you did something you didn't. Don't be a person that always put's them selves in a position to get the credit. Never speak poorly of someone else, no matter how tempting it is. Simply be silent or use an old southern adage, "I really don't know them." If you're talking poorly behind someone's back, the person you're speaking to will think you would do it to them too. Take credit for your

mistakes and vow to never do them again and then don't. See Appendix: "Code of the West."

6. **Time management:** This industry is one of the most time intensive of any I can think of. You're 100% commission compensated. The dollars on each deal are huge. Your time is your own but if you don't use it wisely, your income will suffer. Remember you get back what you put in so using your time wisely is an extremely important factor to your success. Picture that you're at the Staples Center or any indoor sports area and you have 15 minutes to collect as many 1 million dollar bills taped to the bottom of the seats. How would you go about collecting the maximum possible? Would you move fast? Would you hire people to assist you? Etc. Well this business is the process of collecting the million dollar bills. The Staples Center is your territory and the 15 minutes is your career. So here are some tips for being the most efficient million-dollar bill collector.

There are plenty of "Time Management Systems" but they all boil down to the following. The best brokers are always proactive. Don't wait to get your to do's done, go after them with a vengeance. Every evening you must create a "To-Do" list for the next day. You do so primarily so that you're focused and ready to hit the ground running the next day, but also so you can sleep at night. Complete your to- do's in the following order of priority and in the context of the daily schedule below and you'll be ahead of the game.

A) Close or further active deals. Calls, proposals, meetings, etc...
B) Find new opportunity
C) Prepare and execute client presentations and meetings that day. Always maintain current client relationships.
D) Build new business relationships.
E) Build new personal relationships
F) Mundane personal to-do's
G) Things easily delegated

Your daily schedule should be to use your time as follows keeping in mind the priorities above:

7:00-9:00 a.m. is for initiating to-do's, calls and emails, drafting proposals and letters and general paperwork done and handling top priorities so you can focus on the rest of your day and you feel a sense of accomplishment to start the day.

10:00-11:45 a.m. is for cold calling.

11:45-1:30 p.m. is for lunch with a client, college, or potential client as the social time with these people and the information and trust you'll gain is invaluable.

1:30-5:00 p.m. is for cold calling on the phone or by walking buildings in your territory, handing out collateral, closing for meetings or generally building relationships and qualifying prospects for future business.

5:00-6:00 p.m. is for returning phone calls and getting out proposals that have been completed by your assistant.

6:00- 7:00 p.m. is for completing random low priority to do items and writing the next days to do list and prioritizing them for maximum income potential.

If you need a software program to assist there are many out there. My recommendation would be ACT-CRE.

7. **Maintain your energy level:** Get on a healthy routine. Eat right, get plenty of sleep, exercise, have fun.

8. **Maintain your spiritual and emotional health:** Read up on the various methods and choose one for you and make it part of your life.

9. **Reward yourself for a job well done:** Go have a great dinner, take a weekend trip, buy yourself some new business wardrobe items etc.

10. **Keep a running journal:** Mine is a spiral binder but I'm old school. Use whatever system works for you. The purpose is to record notes on every phone call, meeting, and discussion's so you can remember what your action items are and for dispute clarification later if needed.

11. **Communicate in person or by phone:** In this business the best way to get your point across is verbally because of tone, body language, and clear intent.

12. **Answering your phone:** Answer with your full name in an upbeat and direct way with a tone that is customer service oriented and friendly.

13. **Carry and use fully a PDA:** Blackberry is my recommendation.

14. **Keep a clean and organized office:** Being a slob who has a mess everywhere says you have a disorganized mind. There is a lot of paperwork in this business so create a system for keeping it all straight. If you have to pile papers keep the stacks neat by arranging them only by 90 degree angles.

15. **Over prepare for presentations:** Know the client, the assignment, the competition, the location, the order you're presenting, the decision makers and all parties in the room. Call in favors for recommendations prior. Pre-interview with the decision makers. Suggest the agenda by sending a document well in advance. Get to know the players. Find out hidden objections prior to the meeting. Leave nothing to chance! Practice, Practice, Practice!

16. **Meetings:** With rare exception meetings should never go beyond an hour. All parties should have an agenda ahead of time and assignments to bring to the meeting.

17. **Build a list of mentors:** Even though I'll be at the top of your list, always have a mastermind group of mentors you can always call on for opinions.

18. **Be a decision maker:** Weigh all the pros and cons and their long term affects and make the call in short order. Leaders do this well.

19. **Get good rest:** If a problem keeps you awake, write it down and deal with it in the morning. Usually your subconscious will have the answer when you wake.

20. **Know your market better than anyone else and act on the information:** Using Costar, produce lists of every building, building owner, and tenant in your chosen market. Use every weekend, holiday, and day off for whatever time it takes to physically drive, take a photo, and walk into the building lobby to get a feeling for and create a memory of the building. Nobody does this anymore but you will and you'll know your market better.

Study every lease and sale comparable in your market on a weekly basis and commit the deal terms to memory. You'll increase your memory potential and be the undisputed fountainhead of information for your landlords and tenants.

Take all of this information and add it to a Database and CRM. (Customer Relation Management system) A good one is ACT-CRE. Use it religiously to track data, tenant and landlord movement, etc. This tool alone will put you in the top 10% as few have the diligence to keep it up while making prospecting calls etc. Get to know your clients personally. Take them to lunch, dinner, coffee, a bay cruise on your boat, a ski trip, whatever it takes to build a personal relationship. You'll be surprised how many lasting friendships you'll build in the process.

21. **Continued education:** Continuously read and educate yourself on the more advanced techniques and software of the business. When the time comes, attain your CCIM accreditation. It will be invaluable. Read the paper daily for leads. Read the local Business Journal for leads. Always read Commercial real estate periodicals to stay on the top of your game. Learn how businesses run. Learn to read financial statements such as a P&L,

10 Q, and Year-end public financial statement. Research every client before you meet with him or her. They'll be impressed you did your homework. Study negotiating tactics, as these are extremely large deals and your opposing broker or owner has been doing this for a while and will have done their homework on every deal they work on.

22. **Tenant representation deal process:** Become an expert in every aspect of this process and you'll close more deals and make more money. The step-by-step process of the deal pipeline/sales cycle: all scripts, presentation materials, proposals, analytical tools, lease and purchase offer examples etc. are available to you at www.commercialrealestatebrokersacademy.com.

   A. **Prospecting:** Find qualified potential clients by either calling them directly with a list of questions or a general script until you can work extemporaneously. Walk buildings with collateral and ask for the decision maker and qualify them on the spot or close for the qualifying meeting. If you don't get them in person, get a card and follow up with a call and an email with collateral. Afterwards, call and close for the meeting.

   B. **Qualifying:** Learn every intelligent question to ask at the first level of communication to determine if this is an actual potential client. The best place to do this is in person so your first goal while prospecting is to "Close for the meeting." If they aren't available in a short period of time then qualify them on the spot, either while walking their building or on the phone.

   C. **Converting them to a client:** Whether it's by a simple handshake or an "Exclusive Letter of Representation" after presenting against five other competitors, conversion is an art which usually requires a step by step process of convincing the client you have done this many times, are the best in the business, can handle their assignment and they trust you enough to commit to hiring you.

D. **Situation analysis:** Sit with the decision makers after reviewing their lease or ownership situation. Find out what their one, three, and five year business goals are, as well as their financial strength and align a strategy to their stated goals. Perform an employee scatagram with their home zip codes and compare their drive times to the existing facility and consider where the optimal location may be. Be sure you find out where the CEO and other decision makers homes are. 90% of all location decisions take place because of where the owner or top decision maker lives.

E. **Survey alternatives:** Take all the information learned from the situation analysis and come up with a game plan and immediately begin execution on it. This usually means choosing a geographic box and surveying the various available properties that meet their needs within that geographic box. Take that information and format it in an intelligent format, which should also include market information, building information, floor plans, and specific notes on the real situation the building and owner are in which is gathered from the listing broker.

F. **The proposal process:** Select three to five potential alternatives for the client's needs that would all work if they had to. There will naturally be a couple leaders and the client may just want to move forward on his favorite. You always want at least two real back up alternatives as the first choice building may be leased or sold during the process. Additionally, having at least three alternatives in the mix keeps all three owners honest and creates a truly competitive environment among the landlords.

During the proposal process, a few things have to be coordinated to come to terms with a landlord or seller. First, an architectural space plan has to be developed to meet the client's space needs taking into consideration, adjacencies, workflow, space optimization, special use areas, the size of the various offices and work areas. If the deal is at least $5,000, the tenant should interview three space plan firms and choose one that will act as their advocate as the owner will pay for this but the tenant can accurately compare each facility on an apples to apples basis.

Next, it's time to either submit a proposal or LOI (Letter of Intent) on each building calling out all the terms you desire including rent and TI's etc. The alternative (if the deal is large enough) is to submit a "Request for proposal," which creates a psychological turning of the tables. The distancer/pursuer relationship is flipped in your favor and the negotiating dynamic is very different.

Next in the proposal process is to budget the cost of construction to make sure you accurately negotiate the proper budget for construction of interior Tenant Improvements (TI's).

The counter proposal process can go several rounds but ultimately your client will choose an alternative that works. Once you've negotiated to the owner's "point of indifference" there may be several millions of dollars of difference from the beginning of the process to the end and that is a tremendous amount of value you've added for your client. Far surpassing any fee received as part of the deal.

The dynamic is very different if you represent the Owner and your job is to add value through good market information so that he knows when to hold em and knows when to fold em so to speak.

G. **Contract negotiations:** Now you may be negotiating a Lease contract or a Purchase agreement although in either case a strong word of advice: *You're not an attorney and do not give legal advice - ever.* Have a few good Real Estate contract law specialists you work with on a consistent basis and recommend them to your client. They will either use their own attorney or take your advice on your referral, in either case it's your job to perform several specific acts. Some of which are:

i. Compare the LOI to the lease for accuracy of all business terms and dates.

ii.   Work with the client and their attorney to negotiate terms that are not agreeable as his time may cost upwards of $450 per hour.

iii. Introduce industry standard language surrounding building expenses and other market norms that will benefit your client.

iv.   Coordinate the Architect, the attorney, contractor and your client to make sure they are on time and under budget so not to create delays or overage costs that will be billed to your client.

v.   Work closely with the Owner and his attorney to negotiate all terms and assist in overcoming disputes in an amicable way.

H. **The closing process:** Drive all parties to execute the final document. Follow up with exchanging fully executed versions of the final document and follow through with the construction process.

I.   **Payment:** Make sure that payment is made to the brokers of record. If it's a lease, the landlord will need to be invoiced and a check will need to be cut and delivered. If it's a sale, the commissions will have been withheld in Escrow and escrow will issue a check to the Brokers of record upon close of escrow.

23. **Under promise and over deliver:** Do this and you'll always be perceived as the best, and perception is reality.

24. **Be reliable and always follow through:** Do what you say and say what you mean. I cannot over emphasize this enough. Gain this reputation and it will last a lifetime. This is so simple but so effective.

25. **Don't keep secrets from your team:** I am a proponent of being a "no secrets" leader. I make the point that there is no advantage

to keeping secrets and there is a huge benefit to sharing all that you know especially in a team environment. The collective is always smarter than the individual.

26. **Work hard and smart:** They are two different things. Learn the subtleties of each and do both well.

27. **Be meticulous about detail:** "The Devil is in the Details." So is the money!

28. **Be continuously prospecting and adding new business.** You can always hire more employees but you can never hire new clients.

Chapter Seven

Commandment IV: Drink from the Seven Buckets of Revenue

The following are the most recognized revenue lines a broker can tap into. Not every specialty can take advantage of all seven so I will give a real life example of a deal for each, the type of broker that can participate and the math involved in the commissions paid. These are general rules of thumb for today's markets and commissions vary from market to market and from specialty to specialty although these commission examples were taken from real life deals recently. One thing I don't get into in these examples is commission splits. There are too many scenarios to compare so I leave them out. Suffice to say that each deal may have a brokerage house and co broker to split commissions with although not necessarily if you own your own Brokerage firm.

1. Exclusive listing, property for lease: This is a simple case of leasing space in your exclusive listing. You and your team contract with an owner on an exclusive basis to market and lease the owners building. Brokers who perform such transactions are typically, Office, Industrial, or Retail specialists. After extensive marketing and negotiations, the listing team signs a lease for $25,000 for a period of ten years at an average rent of $2.00 over the term.

Example: 25,000 S.F. Tenant, 120-month term of lease, $2.00 average rent/S.F. over the term, 4% commission for the first 5 years and 2% for the second 5 years. The listing broker represents the Tenant.

25,000 S.F. X $2.00 X 60 months X 4%= $120,000
25,000 S.F X $2.00 X 60 months X 2%= $60,000
Total Commissions   **$180,000**

2. Exclusive listing, income property for sale: This is a case where we have a leased building and the owner wants to get the highest value for the building. He has signed an exclusive listing agreement to sell the property. Therefore, you and your team value and prepare an Offering Memorandum, prepare a preliminary flyer for all brokers and buyers to gain initial interest and get it out to your list of all brokers and investors using "Real Capital Markets" (an online buyer database and sales management process software program used in the investment community). Those who show interest receive a detailed Offering Memorandum.

The brokers meet with all interested parties and assist them in understanding the building, the underlying market, and the value of the building. After several buyers make offers and the owner counters and does their diligence to choose the correct buyer, the two parties enter escrow. The buyer does their "Due Diligence," releases their non-refundable deposit and closes escrow on the property. At the close of escrow, the brokers of record are paid through escrow. The brokers who typically participate in these types of transactions are Institutional Investment, Private Client Investment, Hotel Investment, Multi Family Investment, Office, Industrial and Retail specialists.

Example: Building sale price $22,000,000. Broker commissions of 3%.
$22,000,000 X 3 % = $660,000
Total Commissions $660,000

3. Exclusive listing, owner occupied property for sale. This is a situation where the company who occupies the building wants to sell it for one reason or another. You enter into an "Exclusive Listing to Sell" contract. You value the property, market it, take offers, qualify the various buyers, choose a buyer, counter offer, come to terms on a sale, and enter escrow. The seller performs their "Due Diligence," releases their non-refundable deposit and closes escrow. The brokers of record are paid through escrow. The brokers who typically participate in these types of transactions are Institutional Investment, Private Client Investment, Hotel Investment, Office, or Industrial and Retail specialists.

Example: Building sale price: $45,000,000. Broker commissions of 2%. (Typically, as buildings sale prices are larger, the commissions become more negotiable)

$45,000,000 X 2 % = $900,000

Total Commissions $900,000

4. Exclusive tenant representation for lease. In this scenario, you have entered into an "Exclusive Right to Represent" contract with a corporation or Tenant who occupies space. Please refer to the **Tenant Representation Deal Process** section of chapter six and follow all the steps thoroughly. Afterwards, at the collection stage, commissions to the tenant representative broker will be similar to this example. The brokers who typically participate in these types of transactions are Office, or Industrial and Retail specialists.

Example: Your 98,000 S.F. tenant pays an average of $2.20 per square foot for a period of five years. As a result of the market being soft, the owner pays a $2.00 per S.F. bonus for leases longer than three years. Commissions for a five-year lease to the representative broker are 4% of the total rent paid.

98,000 S.F. X $2.20 X 60 Months X 4% = $517,440
98,000 S.F. X $2.00 for Broker Bonus   = $196,000
Total Commissions   **$713,440**

5. Exclusive user/buyer representation to purchase. In this example, you enter into an exclusive representation contract to represent a corporation/user. Typically, these are smaller properties although the commission percentage are usually higher proportionately to the compared to the price. You find the right property for your buyer, then present, negotiate an offer, and agree on terms of the sale. You negotiate a Purchase and Sale Agreement contract, (PSA) and open escrow. You assist with the buildings due diligence. The buyer's deposit becomes non-refundable and escrow closes. The broker of record is paid through escrow. The brokers who typically participate in these types of transactions are Private Client Investment, Office, Industrial and Retail.

Example: Building size 20,000 S.F., Purchase price $275 per S.F., commission 6%.

20,000 S.F. building X $275 per S.F. X 6% = $ 330,000
Total Commissions   **$ 330,000**

6. Corporate sale, lease back. In this scenario you have contracted with the seller to sell a building that they occupy although they will pay the buyer rent to occupy the building for a ten-year period of time and in doing so, creates an income producing property for the buyer. There is a direct correlation to the value of the building based of the capitalized value of the rent and the Internal Rate of Return using a 10 year discounted formula, which most buyers evaluate using software called "Argus." I highly recommend if you intend to sell Investment Grade property that you learn the "Argus" program and have an analyst on your team as an employee or use a freelance analyst as needed per job. In either case, know the program inside and out as your clients surely do. The brokers who typically participate in these types of transactions are Institutional Investment, Private Client Investment, Office, or Industrial and Retail specialists.

Example: 120,000 S.F. building, tenant pays $2.50 Triple Net (NNN) per S.F., over a 10-year term. The buyer agrees to pay a price equal to a 7% capitalization rate on first year income; the first year's rent is $2.10 per S.F. , and the commission is 3%.

120,000 S.F. X $2.10 per S.F. X 12 months divided by .007 = $36,000,000 purchase price X 3% = $1,080,000

Total Commissions	**$1,080,000**

7. Land sale: We saved the easiest for last. We have a parcel of land with a total size of 30 acres for sale. The brokers who typically participate in these types of transactions are Institutional Investment,

Private Client Investment, Hotel Investment, Multi- Family investment, Office, or Industrial and Retail specalists.

Example: There are 43,560 S.F. in each acre and the price is $40 per S.F., with a commission of 5%.

30 X 43,560 X $40 per s.f. X 5%= $2,613,600

Total Commissions	$2,613,600

Each of these examples are highly simplified, and accurately represent commissions paid daily in the real world in this industry. I have a great story of a good friend who just closed a Tenant Representation deal where he represented one of the largest bond funds in America, here in Orange County, California. The deal is for their new world corporate headquarters facility, which is to be built. The deal was negotiated on a ten-year lease and the commissions totaled over $7,000,000 and will be paid in 2011. Congratulations, Rick!

Chapter Eight

Commandment V: Set Measurable Personal, Business, Financial, and Life Goals, then Review Them Quarterly

Setting goals gives you a vision of your future and a pathway to that vision. The process keeps you focused and on track and reviewing them quarterly allows for changes in your life to be integrated smoothly.

Why set goals? So you can clearly and precisely define what you want and then measure your progress.

The process: What do you want for your life? Play out the movie in your head as you would dream it and then set 1, 3, 5 and 10-year goals and life achievements.

The next step is to break them down by categories. Once you see the movie in your head clearly you can go about making the movie a reality. The human brain is an incredible machine. According to studies the brain does not discern the difference between imaginary and real images and scenarios. Furthermore, the brain is always seeking to complete a picture. So set goals and make a habit of viewing your internal movie. What would it *feel* like to obtain those goals? Envision yourself living the life you want. What does it *taste* like? What does it *look* like? Who is there standing next to you? Where are you living? Do this legwork and play this movie in your head constantly. Your brain will naturally seek to complete that picture by manifesting it in reality.

Step 1: Visualize and write down your lifetime goals: Visualizing the movie of your life gives you perspective that shapes your decision making process for life.

The following are the typical categories you should set specific and measurable goals for. You can add or take away from this as your lifestyle dictates.

Business – If this book isn't clear enough about what you should be trying to achieve let me say it again. Become "The Million Dollar Broker."

Financial – These are bigger goals about overall wealth including investments and net worth.

Education – Never stop learning. Become a lifelong learner. Choose your topics and do it.

Personal – Do you want to marry? What type of person is a good choice for you to be your spouse? Do you want children?

Personal expression – Do you want to be a writer, poet, artist etc.?

Mental and emotional – Are you a well-balanced person -- both mentally and emotionally? Are you where you want to be? If not then, find out areas that need improvement, make a plan, and set goals.

Physical health – Athletic, dietary, weight, sports you may want to learn.

Happiness – Measure your overall happiness on a 1-10 scale, 10 being best. Learn ways to increase your happiness and rate it quarterly.

Giving back – How do you make the world a better place? Find ways that fit your lifestyle and capabilities and act on them.

Step 2: When setting goals, work backwards. Start with the end in mind. From your 1, 3, 5, and 10 year goals drill down to quarterly milestones then set to do-lists daily: Make a daily action plan to further each goal by integrating them into your to-do lists so you maintain a balanced, rich life and review the overall results quarterly.

Final advice:

- **Stay the course.** Be diligent and have no excuses.

- **Be specific and precise:** Be able to see, smell, and almost touch your goals mentally. Make them as real to you as possible and try them on for size. Tell someone you're actually doing it. This makes it real.

- **Prioritize:** Just as you do with your everyday to-do's make priorities.

- **Put them in writing:** There is a special power to goals when you write them down and keep doing so every review period.

- **Set Performance goals:** For example, complete 20 cold calls per day, schedule three business lunches per week, give four presentations for new business per month, etc. You'll maintain momentum and feel a sense accomplishment even if the financial goals that should follow have not materialized yet. If you base your goals on personal performance, then you can keep control over the achievement of your goals, and draw satisfaction from the progress.

- **Make all your goals measurable:** Review them and rank your achievements based on a percentage of your goal.

- **Achieving goals:** Take a moment and smell the roses. Reward yourself according to the magnitude of the goal.

Homework: Before you go the next chapter put the book down and do the goal setting exercise I described before picking the book up again. Then put a reminder in your calendar to review them in 90 days and keep doing so.

Chapter Nine

Commandment VI: Be a Person You Can be Proud Of

It's the actions we take on a daily, weekly, and monthly basis that form the habits which determine our level of personal success and ultimately define who we are.

Here are a few things I think are essential to "Be a Person You can be proud of."

1. **Become a leader:** The world requires them. Women respect them. Children need them. Be one and you'll forever respect yourself.

2. **Become independent then interdependent:** First, learn to take care of yourself and to be able to make it on your own. Next, learn to work as an interdependent team. Life is great when you know you can do both.

3. **Have self confidence:** There is a balance one has to have here. Allow yourself to feel confident based on realistic perception of wins you've achieved as you go through life viewed through the perspective of your third eye or ego. Always exude self-confidence, as people will always follow the leader, so to speak. But beware of hubris. If your not familiar with the word or the story, look it up. It has been the demise of many ambitious and young brokers.

4. **Persistence and determination:** Never give up, and never, ever give in. If you stumble and fall, get up, learn from it, and move on. Fall seven times, get up eight. Make this a part of your being.

5. **Think big and imagine bigger:** Read "Think and Grow Rich." Think, Bill Gates, Henry Ford, Rockefeller, Disney, etc....you can do or be anything you can imagine.

6. **Be tough:** Know when to pick your battles but nobody respects a pushover.

7. **Know thyself:** You'll never truly understand others until you know yourself. Be ever diligently introspective.

8. **Be clear about your intentions:** Know exactly what you want down to the smallest detail. Make it known to those that count and then execute.

9. **Focus:** You can have all the drive in the world, but without focus, you'll become lost. The shortest distance between two points is a straight line.

10. **Be forever optimistic:** You always have the choice of looking at your current situation as positive or negative. Always view challenges as opportunities and lessons, and always see your future as an opportunity to become better. Never dwell on the past. Have faith things will always work out for the better.

11. **Passion:** Have a passion for everything you do in life because you believe it's noble. This is a choice. "Perception is reality." Everything about life is better when you put passion behind it. Hold it near and dear to your heart. Never let anyone or anything take it from you.

Even if we aren't conscious of it, it's what we do that determines who we are. And it is ultimately who we are that determines how we react to life's trials and tribulations. So always be a person you can be proud of.

Chapter Ten

Commandment VII: Build Lasting Relationships

Think about some of the similarities between business and personal relationships. They are different but the fundamentals are so similar and one often turns into another so pay attention. Become great at building both and live a rich life. Etiquette and emotional intellect are at the root of both so make sure you study both subjects thoroughly although there are a few points that must be in place to make them last.

Loyalty: According to the Myriam Webster dictionary, "allegiance, faithfulness to commitments and obligations". My #1 requirement of a friend or partner.

Trust: This is the cornerstone to every relationship. Demonstrate that you're trustworthy everyday and you'll receive it in return.

Know your clients and friends: Know every aspect of your relationship base and each specific person intimately.

- Know them personally - their family, friends, where they live, and where they vacation.

- Know the allies and partners they built their empires with. Know how the company was formed, how they structure each deal, and how they philosophically operate their company. Learn how they accomplish their achievements in life.

- Know the company they keep. Be it employee, vendor, or best friend. See what they cherish in people. See if you have those qualities. Know the key employees and make friends or at least be friendly so they know you by name.

- Know their personal interests and if you share them open up and share a part of yourself.

- Be a friend and help with advice or in any way possible, you just might make a best friend out of a client and people like doing business with friends. The greatest gift of this whole process is the possibility of making a new friend as we all need as many as we can get in life.

Communications skills: Stephen Covey put's this well. First, seek to understand then to be understood. That should be the premise of all communication. Although, study communication skills as if your getting your masters degree in it and focus on "**conflict resolution**."

Collaboration: Always conspire to be interdependent with all whom you work with and focus on the win–win and you'll close more deals, therefore making more money while building lasting relationships at the same time.

Give more than you get: people will always want to do business with you.

Chapter Eleven

Commandment VIII: "It's a Marathon not a Sprint"

I put this in quotes because I'm always saying this to my partners, trainees, and friends when a critical stress moment comes or we have a set back or an especially big win over a short-term goal. Like life, this business is a marathon and not a sprint. Don't get too high or too low emotionally as the road of life is long and filled with twists, turns, set back's and big gains just as your career will be in commercial real estate. The idea is run the race. Few people choose to prepare and commit to running a marathon. Most people are bystanders so at lease by committing to this endeavor you have at least chosen to run the race.

There are several parallels and these are the ones I've seen and experienced firsthand:

- First, prepare mentally by visualizing seeing the course in your mind. Where will you begin? Where do you want to be by each stage of the race? Winning is irrelevant as you may be a great racer but there is always someone better so be happy with the fact that you're in the race and achieving your personal goals.

- Train for the race. Every marathoner will tell you that you have to build up your strength and endurance to become great. Look at each day as a training session until you mentally are ready to go when the gun goes off at your starting line.

- Pace yourself. There are mini races within the race and sprinting at certain sections of the course will be required but always remember the greater course and remember you don't want to burn yourself out before the end of the race. The idea is that you have used your energy wisely at each stage of the course and have some left over to reflect and enjoy at the end.

- Along the way, you'll pick up mental skills that you can use later in the race. You'll learn to build buildings. You'll learn to be a master negotiator. You'll learn to become a master conflict resolver etc....These skills can be related to technique but in the long run you can use what you've learned along the way to expand the meaning your life and become a world class "Runner" so to speak.

- If you stumble and fall behind then immediately and calmly get up, access the damage, adjust your mental plan for the race, and thoughtfully continue while learning the lesson of what made you fall and commit to never doing it again. You'll feel a sense of achievement for reentering the race and having learned a lesson along the way.

- If you see another racer fall, go to their aid and help them back into the race. The Karma Gods or whoever will shine upon you later in the race.

- Improve your technique as you continue further into the race, therefore becoming more efficient and running a smarter race.

- Draft off the faster "Runners" in the pack when you need a breather. There is no shame in relying on the racers who are around you who are sprinting to pull you into their draft as the pack is always changing who becomes the leader and it will be your turn several times in the race to lead and pull the pack along.

- Take fuel and liquids along the way. This is giving you the permission to take breaks. Vacations, family time, guy time, girl time, and alone time will all replenish your fuel for the continuing the race. Don't fret. Every smart "Runner" has to do this, or they won't finish the race.

- Take note of your surroundings. Appreciate the bystanders cheering you along, as they are there to support you. They chose to do so. Acknowledge them all along the course and thank them with a smile and a nod, as you'll see many of them you know at the end of the race.

- Form alliances or a team so you run a smarter race and can become part of a greater team. It's always more rewarding when you can experience life with others bonded by a common goal.

- Follow the right path. We've all seen it - the Olympian "Runner" who for one reason or another goes off the course only to realize they will never win nor achieve their goal and they quit the race in tears and disgrace. First, please follow the course set before you. If you go astray momentarily, regroup, ask for directions, and calmly get back on track. The race will be continuing and the point is to be in the race and do your best but never allow your emotions to run too high or too low as this is a Marathon not a sprint.

- Make friends along the way as you're in a pack of people doing what they love. Be friendly to those you're running with you and make a point of getting to know them.

- In life, as in any race, there is always a finish line. You know where it is in your mind roughly. You've trained your entire life for it. It's your ultimate goal so run a race worth being proud of. proud of.

Chapter Twelve

Commandment IX: Have Fun, Save Money and Live a Great Life.

This is the eternal lifestyle vs. saving money balancing act.

How do you balance spending now and saving for later?

First, let me say I'm the right guy for this chapter. At 38 years old, I had a few million in net worth and everything was on cruise control. Literally - my work, income, family, home, boat, trips, investments, savings, and even concerts and sporting tickets were booked a year in advanced by my staff. I had it all in balance and I was having the time of my life. Then came along a little thing called divorce and over the next ten years nothing was the same. Although, I rebuilt well because I did the following. If you do the basics in this business and invest regularly while spending frugally compared to your income and carry little to no debt, then all will be fine. Please speak to a good investment advisor but there are a few very basic principles that you must do.

1. Invest as much as possible in your 401k. If the company matches it, you're making 100% return day 1.

2. Dollar Cost Averaging. Invest an equal amount, monthly into a SEP IRA or directed investment account. Put it into a set of mutual funds that you adjust annually. This will take the highs and lows out of the market as long as you don't ever touch the money until after retirement.

3. Take advantage of the "miracle of compounding interest." Make sure that all of your dividends are reinvested into the Mutual Funds you hold.

4. Invest in Real Estate: Either put the extra money you have set aside for investments into commercial property you know for a fact is a screaming deal. If you don't find any, then purchase

a rental property on a regular basis (let's say every 3-5 years.) In the end, they will become income-producing properties and you'll be collecting checks while on your boat.

Spending vs. saving: Manage it this way:

Savings account A: For having a good time and maintaining the fun factor in your life.

Savings account B: This is for the future, retirement old age when Social Security eventually goes bankrupt.

Remember to set up account B as soon as possible as time is what counts.

- Establish automatic payments on all your debts to make sure you pay everything according to the plan.

- Establish an automatic investment plan for your retirement account that pays yourself first.

- Take out life, disability, and critical illness insurance.

Then, take the money you'll have left over to fund account A, and have fun:

- Buy a cool house in a great neighborhood.

- Buy the car of your dreams.

- Travel to exotic places, buy a boat, learn to skydive, etc. Live life like you mean it!

Account A should be a lot smaller than Account B, and not as restrictive as Account B. This should be a hard and fast rule. The ratio should be 3:1 (B:A).

The answer to the eternal money question is **"Find Your Balance"** because that's what a great life is all about.

Chapter Thirteen

Commandment X: "Give Back"

Through this industry, you'll be given more than you'll ever believe possible. It's all of our duty and responsibilities to remember where we came from not just where we are going. It's all of our responsibilities to help those who have less than us, need a leg up, a kind word, or an opportunity to shine. I was given an opportunity and I want you to give one, too, when the time comes. In addition to mentorship, we all have a greater responsibility to humanity. I'm not particularly religious but these words (which came from some of the greatest thinkers and philanthropists the world has known) say so much about the human condition. I want to share them with you and hopefully have you take away some small sense that we all have a responsibility to "give back."

"The practice of altruism is the authentic way to live as a human being, and it's not just for religious people. As human beings, our purpose is to live meaningful lives, to develop a warm heart. There is meaning in being everyone's friend. The real source of peace amongst our families, friends, and neighbors is love and compassion."
~Dalai Lama

"At the end of life we will not be judged by how many diplomas we have received, how much money we have made, how many great things we have done. We will be judged by 'I was hungry and you gave me food to eat, I was naked and you clothed me, I was homeless and you took me in. Hungry not only for bread, but hungry for love. Naked not only for clothing, but naked for human dignity and respect. Homeless not only for want of a room of bricks -- but homeless because of rejection."
~Mother Teresa

"Everybody can be great...because anybody can serve. You don't have to have a college degree to serve. You don't have to make your subject and verb agree to serve. You only need a heart full of grace. A soul generated by love."
~Martin Luther King, Jr.

"That best portion of a good man's life; his little, nameless, unremembered acts of kindness and love."
~William Wordsworth

"You give but little when you give of your possessions. It is when you give of yourself that you truly give."
~Kahlil Gibran

"No act of kindness, however small, is ever wasted."
~Aesop

"It's every man's obligation to put back into the world at least the equivalent of what he takes out of it. We get a lot, and some take too much. Few give back more than they get - even fewer the equivalent of what they take. There is a mentality of entitlement that has spread throughout the world, and it's selfish appetite is nearly insatiable. Most people are polite, courteous and civil when it serves their self-interest, but not many are truly selfless. When is the last time you did something for another person without expecting anything in return? What difference are you making in the lives of those around you? In your community! In the world! It starts with the little things, but should it stop there? Einstein is probably one of the few whose contributions to society, science and the world could be argued as more than what he got or took, but it doesn't need to be so grandiose to meet his obligation. It all starts with replacing the question, "What do I get?" with "What can I give?" in every situation. Some say, "the more you give the more you get," but I don't think that's true. I think "the more you give the closer you are to even," and as Einstein says, we should at least be striving to break even in this life."
~Albert Einstein

"So long as we love we serve;
So long as we are loved by others,
I would almost say that we are indispensable;
And no one is useless while they have a friend."
~Robert Louis Stevenson

"Thousands of candles can be lighted from a single candle, and the life of the candle will not be shortened. Happiness never decreases by being shared."
~Buddha

"You cannot do a kindness too soon because you never know how soon it will be too late."
~Ralph Waldo Emerson

Chapter Fourteen

Live with No Regrets

Now this journey is coming to an end I want recap where we have been and give you a glimpse into the first steps of your future. We've learned what the lifestyle of the commercial broker can and should be if the work is done properly. We've heard the story of the get rich quick thinkers, how that path leads to failure, and how we should avoid it at all costs.

You learned a bit about my past. The moral of my story is that if given the drive, the will, and the work ethic anyone can overcome adversity and accomplish the goals of this book, which is to make you a million dollar per year gross commission earner in commercial real estate.

We've reviewed the Ten Commandments of being a great broker. In addition, we've chosen where and with whom to work. We've learned that specialization is the key to success, as well as what each of the different specialists does on a consistent basis to be great.

We went deep into the mentality of being the best and all of the best practices of the great brokers and how you can be the best in your market and specialty.

We reviewed the seven different buckets of revenue and how you should take advantage of as many of them as possible, in order to maximize your revenue potential.

We discussed the importance of setting and acting on measurable personal, business, financial, and other life goals and how doing so and reviewing them on a regular basis will set you apart from 95% of people in the world.

We reviewed the importance of building lasting personal and business relationships and how they intertwine throughout your career and life to make your life the richest it can be.

We got into the philosophy of how viewing life as a marathon and not a sprint will give you the right perspective on money, business, relationships and the decision making process when faced with a short tem dilemma that may affect your life for the long run.

We learned that maintaining a balance of hard work, fun and financial responsibility in this industry for the long run will lead to a great life for you and your family.

Finally, we've learned that the big picture of success is to share the gifts that the industry will afford you by being a great person and giving back.

I'm giving you your first action item and **homework assignment**. No excuses. If you don't already have a Real Estate License, apply for the classes and obtain your Real Estate License in your state. It's only a couple of hundred bucks and about four months of light homework in the evenings and your set for life. If you are already a licensed real estate agent your first step is to choose your market and begin calling the office managers of the major firms for the names of the top producers. You will be setting lunch meetings with these brokers to pick their brains to choose a specialty and a home for your future business. DO IT! NO EXCUSES!

One last story to leave you with that is bittersweet for me to tell as not many people have heard this and I haven't thought of it much. But while writing this book I was thinking about the early days of my career, when the rest of my family was basically either poor or the closest thing to it without technically qualifying. I received a call at my office one day.

It was the very somber, almost frantic voice of an oncology nurse in the San Francisco Bay area where my mom was living.

Now a few years earlier, my mom disappeared from our lives when I was a senior in high school. She called me as my senior year was just beginning and we hadn't spoken in months and it happened to be my birthday. As I said earlier in the book, I was an angry teen and there was a silence on the phone after she said, "Hello," and I came back with, "Happy having a kid day!" I could hear her choke up and quietly tear up while trying to maintain her composure. So I sarcastically say it again and she didn't really respond accept to ask for my grandmother. She was at work, I told her, so and the conversation ended with her saying goodbye.

Flash forward nine years later. I'm a 27-year-old, successful junior broker with money in the bank, a nice place to live and a fancy car but my mom had pretty much dropped out of our lives since that call on my 18th birthday. It turns out that she had contracted breast cancer but for some reason didn't want to share it with the family. I can only think that she thought somehow this would burden us. Five years of not hearing from her and not knowing if she was sick or where she lived; I was just pissed that she had completely abandoned me and my brothers, leaving me to be the father figure, so to speak, as I was the oldest of three boys in our immediate family.

She resurfaced in the San Francisco Bay area five years after the call to tell us she had been sick and was ok and living with some guy and that she was happy and in remission. I visited a couple times with my live-in-girlfriend who was from that area and we saw her at her favorite bar a couple of times but it was never the same as when I was a kid and she was actively playing the role (or at least trying to play the role) of mom in my life..

Back to the call from the Oncology nurse and she (in a rushed and somewhat fatalistic voice) says that my family and I need to get there in 24 hours to say "goodbye," as she may not make it through the night. Without a thought, I called the airlines and bought the first flight out for my brothers and me to the bay area where my grandmother, now living in Oregon, met us. My mom was in a coma induced by the Morphine to relieve the pain and the only thing she would or could say was "I love you" repeating it after we would initiate the gesture. Those words were worth the world to me as she passed a few hours later in silence. So that's what I'm left with from her. She at least was able to say goodbye by saying she loved me and that's all I needed.

Now she'll never meet my kids or enjoy holidays or family times again but she will always live in my heart. I remember yelling and swearing at her, saying the smart ass comment about "Happy Having a Kid Day" on my birthday. Now, I wish I could take it back. She was 46 when she died and I'm now 49. My life is dedicated to making sure my kids' lives are better than my and my brothers lives were growing up that I make up for the things I did that I regret and the words I wish I had never said. All I wish now is that I had a mom in my life to share the good times given to me, ultimately, from the chance I was given by my buddy Paul.

Back to you! If you ever thought you could be better and do better for your family while making a mark on the world – now is the time. It doesn't matter if you're a student trying to figure out what your next step is or if you're someone out of work or stuck in a dead end job. Now is your time. The economy can't get much worse. The time for change is happening all over the world and your time to make that change is now. Take the leap. Draw upon your courage, draw up your action plan based on the steps I've given you in this book and go out and change your world and your community. Your greater calling is now.

Never live with the regret that you never took action to make your life or your family's life better. So go do it now! I'll see you on the other side as a colleague with no regrets!

I'd love feedback on my website and would be happy to give further tips to make sure you achieve your ultimate goal. **BUT first complete your homework assignment! Take action!**

www.commercialrealestatebrokeracademy.com

About the Author

Scott Johnstone possesses over 25 years of commercial real estate advisory and brokerage experience, with a total of over $3 billion in transactions. His areas of specialty include corporate tenant representation, acquisition and disposition advisory services, as well as asset marketing and leasing services in Orange County, California. A leader in the industry, he has managed several brokerage teams representing entertainment, technology, financial, Fortune 500 corporate and government clients. Widely recognized for transaction services locally in Orange County, he has also completed numerous complex real estate transactions in major US cities, such as Manhattan, Boston, Los Angeles, Austin, Houston, and San Francisco.

President
Bridge Commercial Properties
January 2011 – Present
Bridge Commercial Properties is a commercial real estate brokerage firm comprised of those dedicated to its core values, which are providing the highest ethical standards while delivering unsurpassed service and market knowledge, thus allowing our clients to make better, faster decisions while reducing their overall cost of operations. Bridge Commercial Properties combines a sole proprietor's attention to detail with institutional experience and knowledge. Scott Johnstone, Bridge's founder, possess over 25 years of commercial real estate advisory and brokerage experience, and have accumulated over $3 billion in transactions. Their areas of specialty include corporate tenant representation, acquisition and disposition advisory services, and asset marketing and leasing services in Orange County, California www.BridgeCommercialProperties.com

Senior Vice President
Grubb & Ellis
2003–2011
Scott was a leader and top-producing broker for the Newport Beach office of Grubb & Ellis with an emphasis on office tenant representation, institutional building marketing, investment sales, medical leasing, and user sales. ***Top Five Office Brokers - Orange County, 2004-2008 ***Top 2 Office Brokers - Newport Beach, 2008.

Grubb & Ellis (NYSE: GBE) is one of the largest and most respected commercial real estate and investment companies in the world. Our 5,200 professionals in more than 100 company- owned and affiliate offices draw from a unique platform of real estate services, practice groups, and investment products to deliver comprehensive, integrated solutions to real estate owners, tenants, and investors. The firm's transaction, management, consulting, and investment services are supported by highly regarded proprietary market research and extensive local expertise. Through its investment management business, the company is a leading sponsor of real estate investment programs.

Co-Founder & Executive Vice-President of Sales & Marketing
TechSpace
2000–2003
Co-Founded in 2000, TechSpace is the nation's premier full-service facilities and infrastructure provider. We integrate world-class flexible office space, state-of-the-art technology services, and business process outsourcing solutions, enabling our customers to focus on their core business. In June 2002, California based Enfrastructure acquired New York based TechSpace, a leading provider of alternative office space and infrastructure services to growing and established companies. In June 2003, Enfrastructure formally changed its name to TechSpace to reflect the company's value proposition and leverage the brand awareness built by TechSpace in other markets throughout the years. www.techSpace.com

Senior Vice President
CB Richard Ellis
1986–2000
Scott acted as a leader and top producing broker focused on Orange County office properties working out of the Newport Beach office of CBRE. CB Richard Ellis is the global leader in real estate services. Together with our partner and affiliate offices, we have more than 300 offices in 50 countries. Each year, we complete thousands of successful assignments with clients from a wide range of industries. Every day, in markets around the globe, we apply our insight, experience, intelligence, and resources to help clients make informed real estate decisions. We do not exist without our clients – and we never lose sight of this fact. To that end, every employee in every office around the world lives by our corporate mission: Put the client first – always. Tailor our services to the client's needs. Think innovatively, but act practically. Help the client make the most informed business decisions. Deliver results. ***South Orange County "Rookie of the year and number 4 in the Office 1988. ***South Orange County Office Broker of the Year, 1993. ***South Orange County Broker of the Year, 1994, 1995, 1996. ***Top 5Brokers of the year South Orange County, 1988-2000. ***Top 10 Office Brokers Orange County, 1989-2000. ***National Chairman's Club Member, 1993, 1994, 1995, 1997.

Commercial
Real Estate
Brokers Academy

2011-Present, Founder, Commercial Real Estate Brokers Academy

Commercial Real Estate Brokers Academy, www.CommercialRealEstateBrokersAcademy.com was founded by Scott Johnstone, a 25 year veteran of the commercial real estate industry, in an effort to create an online, single source of educational products and services for entry level to senior level brokers looking to break into or increase their income in the commercial real estate industry.

Products and services include:

- e-book: The Commercial Real Estate Broker's Career Guide Book
- Paperback Book: Million Dollar Broker: The Commercial Real Estate Sensation
- 6 Disc Audio Training Series: How to Build Your Own Million Dollar Commercial Real Estate Brokerage Firm, a Step-By-Step Process to Building your Own Company the Right Way
- 6 DVD Series: How to Renegotiate a Commercial Real Estate Lease
- Online Video Training Series: Building and Maintaining Your Commercial Brokerage Business at the Highest Level
- Monthly Continuity Membership Video Series: The latest cutting edge presentations, processes and collateral in the commercial brokerage industry, and video interviews with industry leaders on how they became and continue to be great.

Testimonials

"Although Scott is now a competitor, when we worked together years ago when I was still a broker I always found him to be hard working, driven, high Energy and fun to be around."
Jeffrey Moore, Senior Managing Director, CB Richard Ellis

"I had the pleasure of working with Scott when he was a senior level broker at Grubb & Ellis. As one of the Company's top producers, Scott did an excellent job of listening to his clients and developing strategies that exceeded their expectations. He was responsive, creative and productive." April 27, 2011
Robert Bach, SVP, Chief Economist, Grubb & Ellis

"Scott is a true professional in the commercial real estate business. He provided excellent leadership in our effort to find and negotiate office space for the company, and it concluded recently with a very fair and economically advantageous deal for CompPartners. I would definitely work with him again!"
Bruce Carlin, CEO, CompPartners

"Scott Johnstone and I began our careers in Commercial real estate over 25 years ago. Scott is a tenacious broker with a vast knowledge of the Orange County real estate market. He knows how to add value to any transaction. Scott knows how to get the job done, and has an array of testimonials that attest to these facts."
Greg May, Managing Director,
Executive Vice President, Grubb & Ellis

"Scott is a consummate professional who consistently goes beyond what is expected to achieve superior results for his clients. In addition to being incredibly knowledgeable and detail oriented he's a lot of fun to work with!"
Debra Larsen, Co- Founder TechSpace

"Scott is clearly one of the most capable (and therefore successful) commercial real estate brokers with whom I have had the pleasure to work. He and his team of experts were second to none when they represented our interests, particularly when faced with challenging market conditions. I strongly recommend him and would be most pleased to provide further information as may be required in support of this solid professional."

Michael Hall, Ph.D.

"I have known Scott personally and professionally for over 20 years and he is driven, results oriented and has high integrity."

Jim Ulcickas, CEO, Managing partner,
Blue Water Grill restaurants

"Scott has done an excellent job helping us lease and sell our office properties and with our relocation needs."

Lyle McColloch, CFO California Pacific Homes

"Several of my technology clients worked with Scott during their expansion phase and he always impressed with his market knowledge, performance and execution. He is a consummate professional and I would highly recommend him to all of my clients."

Mark Breneman, Senior Vice President,
Silicon Valley Bank

"20 years ago, I got my start in commercial real estate working as a "Runner" for Mr. Johnstone. His passion for the business, strong work ethic and professionalism started me on my career path that I enjoy to this day. Without reservation, I recommend Scott Johnstone for commercial real estate needs."

Chris Schreiber, CCIM,

"Scott's many years in the business of commercial real estate consulting has allowed him to be a trusted and highly credible advisor to many tenant and landlord clients in all aspects of complicated and structured transactions. Scott has worked on some of the largest tenant and landlord projects in Southern California and it's his experience and expertise that makes him very valuable asset in guiding his clients through the transaction process from start to finish. I would highly recommend Scott in the business of commercial real estate transactions."

John Bendetti, Leasing Director, Maguire Properties

"Scott is consistently on top of the market with intimate knowledge of all activity throughout Orange County. He has been a great resource for me and remains a true professional."

Raymond Polverini,
Project Manager CT Realty Investors

"Scott is a consummate professional -- always prepared and polished. He is a strategic thinker, very personable and he instills confidence with his depth of knowledge and expertise."

Ann Forella, Senior Asset Manager,
Buie Stoddard Properties

"Scott is the ONLY commercial real estate broker I recommend. He has impeccable work ethic and his knowledge of commercial real estate in Orange County is remarkable. My father might be the most well connected and reputable commercial real estate individual in Orange County, and he hired and believes in Scott."

Gregory Wertman, Director, "The Buddy Group"

"Scott is experienced, highly personable, very professional and takes great care to listen and provide feasible solutions. Scott is detail oriented, sees the big picture and is a visionary. With compassion for people he is a pleasure to work with."

Stefanie Phan, Assistant Editor, Riviera Magazine

"Scott is a great, hard working, focused, go-getter! He knows whose whom and is focused on getting the job done once he gets the deal. He knows how to work hard and play hard and on top of that is a great dad!"

Stacey Noonan, Account Executive -
Major Accounts Division, Fidelity National Title

"Scott introduced us to several of his clients in which we recommended an audit of the Common Area Maintenance (CAM) charges. We were able to recover overcharges for the clients that most tenants never question. Not only did Scott do the deal, he helped implement the deal after the fact to ensure what was negotiated was actually being done."

Terry Barger, Managing Member, CyberLease, LLC

"I can always count on Scott to get the project leased/sold with expediency and at top value."

John Dobrott, Commercial Developer

"I have worked with Scott on several projects over the years. I've found him to be honest, hard working and diligent with an excellent knowledge of the commercial real estate market in Orange County. He has been a consummate professional in all our various dealings. I highly recommend Scott and look forward to working with him on future investments."

Brent Rusick, President, Buy.com,
CEO Business Cards express

"I have be acquainted with Scott for many years. He is very professional and always delivers for his clients. I would recommend him to any of my clients."

John Racunas, Senior vice president,
Lockton Insurance Brokers

"Scott is an extremely detailed and driven broker. His follow through with his clients places his services above the rest. Scott is a hard worker who somehow finds time to spend with his family. He brings his knowledge of the market and excitement for the industry to each transaction makes working with Scott a pleasure."

Devon Stanke, Property Manager, CIP

"I have known Scott both personally and professionally for many years. Scott has demonstrated constant professionalism, and has always dedicated himself to both his clients and their needs. I look forward to Scott's support on future endeavors."

Gregory Bloom, Executive Vice President &
General Manager, Seal Science, Inc.

"In our dealings with Scott while he was at Grubb & Ellis, we were very impressed with his market knowledge, professionalism and integrity. I would highly recommend him."

> Lonnie Nadal, Commercial Property Investor

"I can't imagine a better client trusted advisor and advocate than you Scott- I really enjoy working with you!" June 29, 2011

> Sandi Warneke, Senior Architect, Gensler

"As a commercial real estate attorney with 30 years+ experience, I have worked with many, many commercial brokers. Scott stands at the top of the list in terms of ability, intelligence and resourcefulness."

> Stevan Gromet, Managing Principal,
> Gromet & Associates

"As a Contractor, we rarely see a broker follow through a project until completion. Scott's attention to detail and diligence on behalf of his clients has been not only helpful, but refreshing to see. I believe this is why Scott maintains one of the best reputations in the business."

> Don Fraser, Vice President, Howard Building Corporation

"Scott, is a very seasoned professional with an attentive eye for detail. "The Devil is in the Detail" Never seems to be a burden for Scott but rather a favorite pastime. Seeking and outing those Devilish clauses is an inherent strength Scott possesses and uses to perfection with each contract." "In addition to Scott being a talented broker he's also an exceptional snowboarder!"

> Ronald McElroy, Owner, Real Office Centers

"Scott has been a great guy to work with. He and his team are organized, knowledgeable and very professional. Our past business deals have been very successful. I recommend Scott to anyone who needs real estate services."

> Ken Wink, Vice President, LEED AP, Ware Malcomb

"I have had the privilege of working with Scott in the past while he was with CBRE. Scott is an exceptional resource, has excellent communication skills, and uses a broad network of business professionals to execute for his clients. I would highly recommend Scott on future assignments. MM"

Michael Merk,

"I have known Scott on both a professional and personal level for over 25 years, and can truthfully say he's a great guy and someone I would look forward to working with on any opportunity. Scott has the unique ability to act in a very professional manner, yet he brings fun and enjoyment to the process at the same time. I'm confident that should someone have the pleasure of working with Scott they would find it to be a very positive experience."

Derek Dean, Sr. Marketing Consultant,
Grubb & Ellis/BRE Commercial

"Scott is a true professional with a high level of integrity! I very much recommend his services."

Trisha Navidzadeh, Space Agent, Virgin Galactic

"Scott has a great team that continues to serve our real estate portfolio at the highest level. When we need an expert, we call Scott and his team. We have know Scott over 20 years, and consider him a valuable asset to our real estate holdings."

Kelly Boyle, Senior Asset Manager,
Griffin Related Properties

"I've worked with Scott at CBRE and he is a conscientious commercial real estate professional. He has always been a top producer and is committed to excellence service and superior market knowledge. He was a real pleasure to work with."

Charlie Christensen, Vice President,
General Growth Properties

"Scott has extensive experience in the commercial real estate field spanning over decades. This combined with his thick Rolodex allows Scott to get deals done at the highest level of execution."

James Fowler, VP, CBRE

"I've worked with Scott on numerous projects where he represented tenants in real estate transactions. Scott has consistently negotiated deals where we clearly saw benefits to the tenant with good TI budgets and aggressive rents. Scott has always been a team player and we certainly enjoy working with him."

Ted Heisler, Senior Architect, Ware Malcolm

"I have had the opportunity to work with Scott several times over the years. Each and every time the end result was positive for all parties. Scott has always exhibited high levels of knowledge, professionalism and integrity."

Dawson Davenport,
President Coldwell Banker Commercial

"Scott has done an excellent job representing Mark IV Capital in South County for many years. Scott is a true professional, possessing expert knowledge, tremendous experience, and creative insight. I would highly recommend Scott to anyone needing quality representation."

Paul Cate, CFO Mark IV Capital

These are my two beautiful children on a farewell trip for my grandmother where we spread her ashes as requested in a secret place on the Merced River in Yosemite National Park. A place we discovered when I was a child on one of our many camping trips in this magnificent valley. A place where the mighty Merced slows to a peaceful flow , mirroring the granite walls of the valley where there is a rock in the slow waters flow. "The rock" that we all swim to and warm ourselves on after the snow melted waters chill our bones. The rock that seems to have avoided times eventual test. A place where I take my children now and where we bid our final farewell.

Here is a poem my grandmother wrote about me some years ago that she published shortly after her last birthday at the age of 89. We didn't have a lot of money as kids and camping was our favorite vacation time.

Boy At The End Of The Pier

The sun sinks below the rim of the sea.
The shoreline and the Gaviota Hills

Blur as misty vapor fills the early evening air.
The water and the sky are darkening, swells break
Heavily against the wooden struts and spans.
The boy was the only one still fishing,
The only one on the end of the pier.
Skinny twelve-year-old kid, sunburned,
Yellow hair stiff with salt, eyeballs pink
From the wind and flashes from the sunstruck sea.
He's been here since early morning,
Before the fog lifted, except for runs
To the rest room on the beach, or
The faucet on the pier for brackish water.
A blue plastic bucket holds the day's catch,
Four sand dabs and two silver mackerel,
One still splashing in the bloody water.
A couple of trash fish lie by the pail,
Chopped up for bait, fish blood and
Stringy entrails now dried, becoming
An integral part of the wooden deck
Till the next storm washes it clean.
An oblong plastic container
Holds rusty pliers, a red penknife,
And a square of plastic sponge
Pierced by odd sized hooks.
On the smooth, gray planks around him
Are curled up remnants of peanut butter sandwich,
Pieces of orange rind and three empty Coke cans,
A Milky Way wrapped and a Frito bag,
All covered with sand and fish scales.
Two old men in dark zippered jackets and
Baseball caps clean their fish in
A trough by a faucet, glancing at
The boy casting his line against the wind.
They nod their heads approvingly -- tough little kid.
One by one, the lights go on
In the RV park across the beach.
A woman leaves a campsite, crosses

The windblown sand stinging like sleet,
Head down, body braced against the wind,
She walks quickly to the end of the pier.
She embraces the boy and he pulls up his line,
Secures the hook to the bail of the reel.
Slowly and reluctantly, he follows her,
Looking back over his shoulder
At the dark blue sea.
It is his passion.
He'll be back in the morning.

Marilynn P. Ellis

Appendix

A. "Broker Code of the West"

B. Example: Exclusive Tenant Representation Letter

C. Example: Office – Request for Proposal-RFP

D. Example: Office – Letter of Intent-LOI

E. Example: Office – User-Purchase, Letter of Intent-LOI

F. Example: Office – Investor-Purchase, Letter of Intent-LOI

G. Example: Deal Timeline & Flowchart

H. Example: Capabilities Brochure – Tenant

I. Example: Market Newsletter

Appendix A: "Broker Code of the West"

The definitive code of Ethics passed down from leader to leader, firm to firm.

I. Commercial Real Estate Brokerage Practices

A. Initial Contact - Clients

When initially contacting a potential client, the client must be asked if he is working with any other broker within your office. If he mentions another broker at your office, it should be immediately determined (a) who the other salesperson is, and (b) whether this is a current relationship and specifically involved with the client's current requirement. Should this be the case, it's improper to continue, and the second salesperson should state that the client is "in good hands" and then immediately inform the original salesperson of the contact.

B. Different Decision Makers

In some cases, two or more salespersons may learn that they are working independently with different decision makers within the same firm. When first learning of the situation, they are encouraged to "pool their efforts." Should that not occur, once all salespersons involved have discussed it fully with each other, they are obligated to immediately inform management of the problem, who, in turn, shall render a decision as to who shall represent the client.

C. Prior Relationships

If a salesperson leases or sells a building to a client, he shall have no automatic right to represent that client on future transactions. It should be noted, however, that it might be beneficial to all parties to honor another salesperson's prior relationship.

D. Expired Listing Protection

When an exclusive listing expires or is cancelled and the contract is not given to another salesperson, the listing salesperson shall be honored as the exclusive agent within the firm for an additional period of sixty days, if the listing salesperson has been actively marketing the property during the original listing period.

   E. Injecting Oneself in Deal

Under no circumstances should a salesperson try to inject himself into a transaction initiated by another broker from the same firm.

II. Co-Listings

A. Listings, which are serviced by two or more salespersons, merit an acknowledgement of the commission split on both the seller/lessor side and buyer/lessee side, ideally in writing. Variations and exceptions must be clarified "up front," in writing, signed by all parties and could include:

1. Exclusions of previous clients.
2. Different treatment for "call-ins" versus "cold calls."
3. Properties where one of the salespersons is operating outside his geographical territory.
4. Any commission split other than an equal distribution among members.

III. Partnership / Teams

A. It's recommended that the partnerships or teams address, in advance and in writing, such issues as the following:

1. Purpose of the partnership/team.
2. Expected duration.
3. Treatment of deals resulting from partnership/team activities but not related to the designated requirement.
4. Representation of prospects after partnership/team termination.

B. As a guideline, a partnership or team, when joining another salesperson(s), shall be treated as one person, regardless of the number of salespersons in the partnership/team. Understandings should be evidenced by written agreement.

IV. General

A. Seven-Day Grace Period

A salesperson will have a period of seven (7) calendar days after taking a valid listing to present the listing to his prospective buyers/tenants. At the end of that period, he or she must distribute the listing in the normal manner.

B. Dissatisfied Client

Should a client inform one salesperson that or she is unhappy with the services of another salesperson, the second salesperson should immediately inform the original salesperson and management.

C. Open Listings

Management must approve all open listings. It's the obligation of the listing salesperson to distribute the information within the appropriate offices in order to be honored as the listing agent within the same firm. However, this listing position does not apply to major properties, such as development projects, which are generally known to be available.

V. Negative Selling

A. Sales personnel shall not use "negative selling" in an attempt to gain control of a client or property. Such tactics include implying (or expressly stating) that another broker/salesperson, or office in the same firm, is not sufficiently qualified by experience or location to handle a particular requirement.

VI. Offers

A. Once an offer has been presented and accepted, no further offers should be solicited. One has a duty to inform all parties they may represent and receive approval from the parties in writing when one is in a situation to present multiple offers on one property.

VII. Sharing Information – Handling Potential Disputes

A. Sales personnel are encouraged to share information freely. If a salesperson expects to be compensated for sharing specific information (or clients), it's his or her duty to be explicit about their commission expectations. Any understandings between salespersons shall be reduced to writing and signed by all parties.

B. Should any information be relayed to another broker within your office in or out of the specialty group meetings and the receiving broker learns differently about the information it should be relayed immediately to the broker providing the information and all questions should be directed to the information source before going direct to the client.

C. Should situations arise that cause conflict and or confusion, the brokers involved should immediately bring it to the attention of the other to "politely discuss" each side before going to management.

VIII. Contact with Potential Clients

A. Initial Contact — if a broker/salesperson in your firm is mentioned:

1. If actively working together: "You're in good hands."
2. Recommendation: Talk to the salesperson, tell them you "stumbled on" their deal and ask if you can be of any assistance.
3. If not active: "I'll speak with _____ and one of us will get back to you."
4. Recommendation: Team up!

B. Different Decision-Makers — do as the code says. What should be prevented is broker/salespeople hearing of a requirement and purposely go to a different decision-maker — this is highly unethical.

C. Whom Can You Call? Anyone who is not currently known to be working with a broker/salesperson in the same firm — at your discretion — no one who recently worked with a broker / salesperson in your firm.

IX. Hot Off the Press / Marketing Materials

A. Do not review other brokers printed materials without the marketing broker's permission and refrain from approaching in-house agents unsolicited about properties that they have not yet openly marketed (aka "surfing the copy machine for leads"). Often time's agents are given permission to discreetly or even exclusively market an asset. However, out of respect to the agent that generated the opportunity, please do not approach the marketing broker until such times as he sends out an announcement encouraging others to participate in the process.

B. An exception might be a situation where a project handled by another broker (i.e. leasing broker) is being marketed by another broker within the company, without the leasing agents involvement and our company comes off as being uncoordinated in our marketing efforts as a prospect might ask the leasing agent about a property he thinks the agent would naturally know is being offered for sale or lease. In this case, the discovering agent should first approach the marketing broker and then management if the situation is "murky."

X. Other Issues
A. Dissemination of Information
Don't mail information to other people's clients.

B. Runner / Trainer Relationship
As a "Runner", if you uncover a deal or create a relationship, it's the property of your trainer.

C. Promotion of Fellow Salespeople
Always promote a broker/salesperson in your firm for listings and tenant representation assignments!

D. Full Commission and Bonus Commissions
Don't ask for them and don't encourage your clients to give them unless absolutely necessary to get the project leased — don't accept them when offered to you unless they are being formally offered to the entire community.

E. Direct Contact with Other's Clients
Don't contact your counterparts' clients in a deal, unless your counterpart gives you permission.

F. Soliciting listed Buildings

The real estate code of ethics strongly prohibits soliciting already listed buildings.

G. Plagiarism

Always respect the creator of unique marketing tools. Ask permission to copy something exclusive to them — especially if they were your trainer.

H. Renegotiation of Lease Extensions and Options

If a contract exists, you should always ask, especially if a fellow broker/salesperson is involved, work on the deal at your risk without potential for payment.

I. Appraiser Calls

Always support a fellow salesperson if an appraiser calls on one of their deals.

J. Investment – Lease Scoop

Never try to scoop a salesperson leasing a building by trying to sell it as an investment before they can — after all, they created the opportunity by leasing it.

K. Owner – Tenant Conflict

If a salesperson is representing a tenant on relocation, don't call the landlord to solicit the listing without asking the salesperson first. You may screw up their deal and they should have a chance at the listing — unless, of course, you have a relationship with the landlord on the building and your firm does not list it.

L. Past Discussions on Opportunities

Comments like "let's go after…" or "let's work on…" should be documented or have a formal/verbal agreement unless both parties actively pursue the deal with regular discussion. Too often, after nothing has happened, one party will be reintroduced to the deal by another salesperson, work on the deal with them, and be accused by the old partner of cheating them.

M.   Office Talk

You can't work on anything you overhear that wasn't addressed to you. Respect an open environment — it's a privilege.

N. Administrative Support Desks

If you oversee something regarding someone else's business while at your administrative support's desk — erase it from memory.

O. Sign Calls

Partners on the listing referenced share all sign call deals.

P. Verbal Registration

Don't discuss a deal in hopes of getting others to back off. Unless you have a solidified relationship — or have had a meeting with the principal — you speak at your own risk.

Q. Simultaneous Pursuit of a Deal - Options
- Team up
- Continue until one party gets control — fairly
- See your manager —, which is always a good idea first.

R. Listings

If a salesperson has a lease listing, you can't call the owner regarding a sale.

S. Exclusivity of Clients Listing to Listing

This is a gray area — always honor current relationship and be fair to your fellow salespeople — use the relationship to your advantage

T. Seniority

Respect the senior salespeople, even though they may be no older than you
- It takes a lot to be successful here in the long run, and they have earned it
- Besides, they have probably helped you along the way and you'll be senior yourself one day.

U. Brokerage Team Restructuring

If multiple salespeople from the same firm are working together on the same account, and one or more salespeople desire to either add a different salesperson, or otherwise restructure the current team, the salesperson initiating the change shall initially discuss the desired change with the current team and then if necessary with management. In no event shall a salesperson initiate any discussion with a client unless and until it has been resolved as outlined above.

Appendix B: Example Document - Exclusive Tenant Representation Letter

ACME WIDGIT CORPORATION

January 1, 2011

Scott Johnstone
Bridge Commercial Properties
4695 MacArthur Blvd, Ste 1100
Newport Beach, CA 92660

John Doe
CEO
ACME Widgit Corporation
1000 Commonwealth Blvd.
Newport Beach, CA 92660

949.555.5555 main
949.555.5555 fax

RE: ACME Widget Company Representation:

This letter confirms the agreement between ACME Widget Company and Bridge Commercial Properties as its sole and exclusive agent to aid in a contemplated relocation, renewal, or purchase of a facility.

This appointment shall become effective immediately and shall extend until a lease, lease amendment, sublease, or set of escrow instructions is fully executed. It is to be understood that either party upon thirty (30) days written notice may cancel this agreement. In such event, Bridge Commercial Properties shall be protected on all properties submitted.

Bridge Commercial Properties is authorized to negotiate on behalf of Acme Widget Company with owners, developers, brokers, and all interested parties to explore real estate opportunities that meet ACME Widget Company.

Bridge Commercial Properties will make all efforts to present to ACME Widget Company all pertinent information in detail as required throughout the decision making and transaction process.

All documentation resulting from Bridge Commercial Properties efforts and negotiations is subject to ultimate approval by ACME Widget Company.

Commissions and/or fees to which Bridge Commercial Properties is entitled shall be paid by the owner, landlord, or sub-landlord of the property purchased, leased, or subleased by ACME Widget Company shall require that the owner, landlord, or sub-Landlord compensate Bridge Commercial Properties with a market commission.

AGREED AND ACCEPTED:

ACME Widget Company   Bridge Commercial Properties
By: _____   By _____

Appendix C: Example Document – Office – Request for Proposal-RFP

January 1, 2011

Scott W Johnstone
President
Bridge Commercial Properties
4695 MacArthur Court, Ste 1100
Newport Beach, CA 92660

949.555.5555 main
949.555.5555 fax
S@BridgeCommercialProperties.com
www.BridgeCommercialProperties.com

John Doe
Any Brokerage Company USA
12345 Any Street, Suite 100
Newport Beach, CA 92660
VIA EMAIL: johndoe@anybroker.com

RE: **REQUEST FOR PROPOSAL TO LEASE 111 #1 STREET, NEWPORT BEACH, CA**

Dear Tim:

On behalf of The Acme Corporation, ("Tenant"), Bridge Commercial Properties has been authorized to present the following Request for Proposal to Any Landlord ("Landlord"), whereby Tenant would consider leasing space at 111 #1 Street, Newport Beach, CA (the "Project").

The terms and conditions Tenant requests Landlord to respond to are as follows:

1.	**Project:**	111 Plaza
2.	**Premises:**	111 #1 Street, Newport Beach, CA
3.	**Square Footage:**	Approximately 50,000 rentable square feet. All measurements, including those described above, are to be determined in accordance with the standards set forth in ANSI Z65.1-1996, as promulgated by the Building Owners and Managers Association ("BOMA Standard"). Tenant shall be entitled to independently verify all measurements.

4. **Lease Term:**	Please provide a ten (10) year option.
5. **Lease Commencement Date:**	The Lease Term shall commence upon substantial completion of the Tenant Improvements (as described below) and after a final certificate of occupancy has been issued with respect thereto, anticipated to be July 1, 2011.
6. **Delayed Occupancy Resulting from Landlord Delays:**	In the event the Tenant Improvements are not substantially complete for move in by Tenant on or before sixty (60) days from the Target Commencement Date, Landlord shall indemnify and hold Tenant harmless against any damages, cost for liabilities incurred by Tenant including but not limited to additional rent and/or penalties resulting from such delay.
7. **Early Occupancy:**	Following completion of the Tenant Improvements, subject to a punch list, Landlord shall deliver a Certificate of Occupancy to Tenant and grant a period of two (2) weeks prior occupancy to fixturize the Premises which would include, but not limited to, installation of furniture systems, fixtures, and equipment (FF&E), telecommunications and computer cabling.
8. **Rental Rate:**	Please propose the basic monthly rental rate during the lease term on a full service gross basis.
9. **Tenant Improvements:**	Tenant requests that Landlord provide Tenant with a tenant improvement allowance sufficient to cover all costs associated with the build-out. The tenant improvement costs may include, but shall not be limited to, the following: space planning, programming, design development drawings, pricing drawings, construction drawings, electrical / mechanical / plumbing / engineering drawings, reimbursables, city permits, approval fees, construction administration, construction, all profit, overhead and general conditions.
10. **Core and Shell Description:**	Tenant requests that Landlord provide written information as it relates to the condition of the core and shell.

11. Move Costs, Telephone/ Computer Cabling Costs, And FF&E:	Tenant will require Landlord provide an allowance, which will be used to assist Tenant with its move costs, telephone/computer cabling costs, and FF&E.
12. Option to Renew:	So long as Tenant is not in default under the terms of the lease and with not more than nine (9) months and no less than six (6) months prior written notice, Tenant shall have the option to renew the lease for two (2) additional periods of five (5) years each. The rent during the option term shall be 95% of the then fair market value for similar type properties in the general market area.
13. Operating Expenses:	Tenant shall pay its pro rata share of operation expenses and real estate taxes ("Operating Expenses") associated with the Premises, in excess of the base year amount. The base year of the lease for the purposes of calculation shall be 2012. The base year shall be grossed up to reflect 100% occupancy of the Project and any increases in operating expenses shall be capped on a non-cumulative, non-compounded basis at three percent (3%) per year. In addition, Tenant will require a list of operating expense exclusions to be incorporated into the lease agreement.
14. Audit by Tenant:	Landlord shall provide to Tenant in substantial detail each year, calculations performed to determine the Project Operating Expenses in accordance with the applicable provisions of the lease. Landlord shall show by account the total operating costs for the building and all adjustments corresponding to the requirements as set forth herein. Landlord shall provide in reasonable detail its calculation of Tenant's pro rata share of project operating expenses by setting forth the ratio of the Premises, ratable square feet to project's rentable square feet. Landlord shall also provide the average building occupancy for such year.

Tenant shall have the right, at its own cost and expense (without requiring that Tenant pay Landlord's cost of complying with this provision) to audit or inspect Landlord's detailed records each year with respect to the project operating expenses as well as other additional rent payable by Tenant pursuant to the lease for any lease year (not to exceed one time per year). Landlord shall utilize, and cost utilized, accounting records and procedures for each lease year conforming to generally accepted accounting principles, consistently applied with respect to all project operating expenses for such lease year.

15. First Right of Refusal: Tenant shall have the First Right of Refusal to lease any space that may become available in the building. When any space becomes available and Landlord has a bona fide interested third party, then landlord shall provide Tenant with written notification of such availability and Tenant shall have ten (10) business days to elect to expand into said Expansion Space. Expansion Space terms and conditions shall be co-terminus and consistent with the terms and conditions originally negotiated for the initial Premises incorporating a new base year for the purposes of Operating Expenses calculation.

16. Relocation: Landlord shall have no right to relocate Tenant's Premises during the Lease Term.

17. Parking: Tenant shall have, for the use of Tenant and its clients and employees and other agents, a parking ratio of four (4) parking spaces per one thousand (1,000) rentable square feet leased. All Tenant's parking spaces shall be available free of charge and accessible 24 hours per day, seven (7) days per week, every day of the year for the entire term of the Lease and any extensions thereafter.

18. Roof Rights:	Tenant shall have the exclusive rights to install and maintain on the roof of the building, satellite dishes for Tenant's exclusive use. The location of such equipment shall be in a mutually agreed upon location with specifications being provided by Tenant for Landlord's reasonable review and approval. Landlord shall not charge Tenant for said rights and Tenant shall be responsible for the installation, maintenance, including electricity, insurance and removal of said satellite, including the damage to the building, if any, caused by the use or installation of said satellite.
19. Architects/Space Planning:	In the event your building is selected as a finalist, Tenant will require that Landlord compensate an architect of Tenant's choice to complete a space program, space plan and design development drawings at the cost of $0.15 per usable square foot. Tenant's architect shall complete all space programming, space planning, and construction drawings as well as coordinating all electrical, mechanical, plumbing, and engineering drawings.
20. Construction Administration Fee:	There shall be no construction administration fee of any kind.
21. Heating, Ventilation & Air Conditioning ("HVAC"):	Tenant's standard operating hours during the term of the lease shall be Monday through Friday, 6:00 a.m. to 8:00 p.m., and Saturday, 8:00 a.m. to 1:00 p.m. After hours HVAC shall be provided at Landlord's actual cost.
22. Toxic Materials:	Landlord shall have the express responsibility to advise Tenant of any toxic materials or hazardous wastes, which are located in, or about the Premises.

23. Non-Disturbance Agreement:	Landlord shall provide Tenant with a non-disturbance agreement reasonably acceptable to Tenant from any superior mortgagee of Landlord now and when that may come into existence at any time prior to the expiration of the term of the lease as a condition precedent to any obligation of Tenant to subordinate its interest to any such person.
24. Insurance and Indemnity:	Landlord shall maintain full replacement "all risk" property insurance on the Project with full waiver of subrogation and shall indemnify Tenant on the same terms as Tenant may agree to indemnify Landlord.
25. Property management and Project Defects:	Landlord, at Landlord's sole cost and expense, shall operate, manage, and maintain the Project and common areas in first class order, condition and repair throughout the lease term. Landlord shall be 100% responsible for repair of any and all defects in the Project and Premises over the lease term.
26. Americans with Disabilities Act:	All costs related to compliance with the applicable provisions of the Americans with Disabilities Act of 1990 (ADA) shall be Landlord's cost. These costs shall not be part of the Tenant Improvement Allowance or contribute to increasing the operating expenses.
27. Signage:	In addition to suite entry and directory board signage, Tenant will require the right, but not he obligation, to install building top and monument signage at the Project.
28. Sublease/Assignment:	Tenant shall have the right to sublease or assign all or a portion of the space to any subsidiary company without Landlord's approval and all other subleases or assignments with Landlord's approval, which shall not be unreasonably withheld, conditioned or delayed.

29. Security Deposit:	Tenant shall not be required to pay a security deposit.
30. Holding Over	In the event Tenant remains an occupant of the Premises beyond the expiration of the lease term, Tenant will agree to pay Landlord a hold over rent in the amount equal to 150% of the then rent payable.
31. Commission Agreement:	Bridge Commercial Properties is representing the Tenant in this possible transaction, and shall be paid a standard full commission of four percent (4%) for the first five (5) years, and two percent (2%) for the second five year of the full service gross lease value by Landlord as follows: One hundred percent (100%) is payable upon lease execution.
32. Dual Agency Disclosure:	In the Agreement, Lessor and Lessee will each represent and warrant to the other that it has engaged no broker or intermediary other than Bridge Commercial Properties, which represents both the Lessor and Lessee, in connection with the proposed transaction and will agree to indemnify the other party for any other loss, liability, and reasonable expenses, including attorneys' fees, incurred by virtue of any action on its part giving rise to a breach of such warranty or a claim for such other fees. Lessor will be responsible for commission due to Bridge Commercial Properties pursuant to a separate written agreement.
	Both parties are hereby notified of the Dual Agency and agree hereto.

This Proposal is intended solely as a preliminary expression of general intentions and is to be used for discussion purposes only. The parties intend that neither shall have any contractual obligations to the other with respect to the matters referred herein unless and until a definitive agreement has been fully executed and delivered by the parties. The parties agree that this Proposal is not intended to create any agreement or obligation by either party to negotiate a definitive lease/purchase and sale agreement and imposes no duty whatsoever on either party to continue negotiations, including without limitation, any obligation to negotiate in good faith or in any way other than at arm's length. Prior to delivery of a definitive executed agreement, and without any liability to the other party, either party may (1) propose different terms from those summarized herein, (2) enter into negotiations with other parties, and/or (3) unilaterally terminate all negotiations with the other party hereto.

We appreciate your assistance and cooperation, and look forward to receiving your response. This Proposal shall remain valid until **January 10, 2011**. If you have any questions, please feel free to contact either of us at your convenience.

Regards,

Scott W. Johnstone
Senior Vice President
(949) 555-5555
s@BridgeCommercialProperties.com
CA License # 00950979

cc: Robert Rich, CEO, Acme Corporation

EXHIBIT A

CALIFORNIA SALE/LEASE AMERICANS WITH DISABILITIES ACT, HAZARDOUS MATERIALS AND TAX DISCLOSURE

The Americans with Disabilities Act is intended to make many business establishments equally accessible to persons with a variety of disabilities; modifications to real property may be required. State and local laws also may mandate changes. The real estate brokers in this transaction are not qualified to advise you as to what, if any, changes may be required now, or in the future. Owners and tenants should consult attorneys and qualified design professionals of their choice for information regarding these matters. Real estate brokers cannot determine which attorneys or design professionals have the appropriate expertise in this area.

Various construction materials may contain items that have been or may be in the future be determined to be hazardous (toxic) or undesirable and may need to be specifically treated/handled or removed. For example, some transformers and other electrical components contain PCBs, and asbestos has been used in components such as fire-proofing, heating and cooling systems, air duct installation, spray-on and tile acoustical materials, linoleum, floor tiles, roofing, dry wall and plaster. Due to prior uses of the Property or in the area, the Property may have hazardous or undesirable metals (including lead-based paint), minerals, chemicals, hydrocarbons, or biological hazards (including, but not limited to, mold) or radioactive items (including electrical and magnetic fields) in soils, water building components, above or below-ground containers or elsewhere in areas that may or may not be accessible or noticeable. Such items may leak or otherwise be elsewhere in areas that may or may not be accessible or noticeable. Such items may leak or otherwise be released. Real estate agents have no expertise in the detection or correction or hazardous or undesirable items. Expert inspections are necessary. Current or future laws may require clean up by pas, present and/ or future owners and/or operators. It is the responsibility of the Seller/Lessor and the Buyer/Tenant to retain qualified experts to detect and correct such maters and to consult with legal counsel of their choice to determine what provisions, if any, they may include in transaction documents regarding the Property.

Sellers/Lessors are required under California Health and Safety Code Section 25915 et seq., to disclose reports and surveys regarding asbestos to certain persons, including their employees, contractors, co-owners, purchasers and tenants. Buyers/Tenants have similar disclosure obligations. Sellers/Lessors and Buyers/Tenants have additional hazardous materials disclosure responsibilities to each other under California Health and safety Code Section 25359.7 and other California laws. Consult your attorney regarding this matter, and make proper disclosures. Grubb & Ellis Company is not qualified to assist you in this matter or provide you with other legal or tax advice.

Sale, lease and other transactions can have local, state and federal tax consequences for the seller/lessor and/or buyer/tenant. In the event of a sale, Internal Revenue Cod Section 1445 requires that all buyers of an interest in any real property located in the United States must withhold and pay over to the Internal Revenue Service (IRS) an amount equal to ten percent (10%) of the gross sales price within ten (10) days of the date of the sale unless the buyer can adequately establish that the seller was not a foreigner, generally by having the seller sign a Non-Foreign Seller Certificate. Note that depending upon the structure of the transaction, the tax withholding liability could exceed the net cash proceeds to be paid to the seller at closing. California poses an additional withholding requirement equal to three and one-third percent (3 1/3%) of the gross sales price not only on foreign sellers but also out of state sellers and sellers leaving the state if the sale price exceeds $100,000. Generally, withholding is required if the sales proceeds are distributed outside of California, if the last known address of the seller is outside of California or if a financial intermediary is used. Consult your tax and legal advisor. Real estate brokers are not qualified to give legal or tax advice or to determine whether any other person is properly qualified to provide legal or tax advice.

SELLOR/LESSOR   **BUYER/TENANT**

By: _____   By:_____

Title: _____   Title: _____

Date: _____   Date: _____

Appendix D: Example Document – Office Lease Letter of Intent-LOI

BRIDGE
COMMERCIAL PROPERTIES

Scott W Johnstone
President
Bridge Commercial Properties
4695 MacArthur Court, Ste 1100
Newport Beach, CA 92660

949.555.5555 main
949.555.5555 fax
S@BridgeCommercialProperties.com
www.BridgeCommercialProperties.com

January 1, 2011

Jan 1, 2011
John Doe
Any Brokerage Company USA
12345 Any Street, Suite 100
Newport Beach, CA 92660
VIA EMAIL: johndoe@
anybroker.com

Delivered by email:
johndoe@anybroker.com

RE: Request For Proposal to Lease
**   111 #1 Street, Newport Beach, CA**

Dear John:

On behalf of Acme Corporation ("Tenant"), we have been authorized to present this best and final lease counter proposal for your consideration. The following sets forth a summary of the terms and conditions under which the tenant would enter into a lease for the above-referenced property.

1. Tenant:	Acme Corporation
2. Building:	111 #1 Street, Newport Beach, Suite 100 Newport Beach, California 92660
3. Premises:	Approximately 10,000 rentable square feet located in Suite 100 of the building ("premises"). Final square footage to be determined following approval of space plans.
4. Term:	Sixty-Six (66) months.
5. Commencement:	Upon substantial completion of tenant improvements.
6. Moving Allowance:	Tenant shall receive a two-dollar ($2) per rentable square foot moving allowance.

7. Early Access:	Tenant shall be granted access to the premises up to fourteen (14) days prior to the commencement of the lease term free of all charges for the purposes of installing phone/data lines and furniture.
8. Base Rental Rate:	Rent shall be calculated on a full service gross basis as follows:

Month(s)	Monthly rent per square foot
1	$1.80
2-11	$0.90
12	$1.80
13-24	$1.90
25-36	$2.00
37-48	$2.10
49-60	$2.20
61-66	$2.30

9. Operating Expenses:	Tenant shall pay its proportionate share of operating expenses and real estate taxes ("operating expenses") associated with the premises, in excess of the base year amount. The base year of the lease for the purposes of calculation shall be 2012. Tenant shall be excused from operating expense escalations for the initial twelve (12) months of the lease term. The term "proportionate share" shall be defined through an equation in which the numerator shall be the number of rentable square feet of floor area in the premises and the denominator of which shall be the number of rentable square feet of all rentable square footage within the project. Operating expenses, taxes, insurance, and utilities shall be calculated with the standard accounting practices based on the building being ninety-five percent (95%) occupied. Tenant shall have industry standard audit rights of landlord's operating expense accounting. A cap of four percent (4%) shall be instituted on annual operating expense increases over and above the prior year's billing. The four percent (4%) shall be based upon the total operating expenses for the project, of which, tenant shall pay its pro-rata share.

10. Tenant Improvements:	Landlord shall provide a tenant improvement allowance equal to $30.00 per rentable square foot or turnkey, whichever is greater. If the tenant improvement allowance is less than $30.00 per square foot, tenant shall have the right to apply balance to offset rent, FF&E, and parking.
11. Tenant Signage:	Landlord shall provide, at landlord's cost, building standard directory and suite signage for tenant. Additionally, landlord should provide at tenants cost monument signage for the project.
12. Parking:	Tenant shall be allotted four (4) spaces per one thousand (1,000) rentable square feet including two (2) reserved stalls free for the term. Parking shall be free for the term.
13. Assignment & Subletting:	Any consent required for assignment of subletting shall not be unreasonably withheld or delayed by landlord. Landlord will have no recapture rights, and tenant will be allowed to retain all, if any profits. Tenant shall have the right to sublet or assign to a parent or, subsidiary or affiliate without landlord consent. Tenant shall be entitled to sublease any or all of the premises.
14. Heating, Ventilating & Air Conditioning:	The normal operating hours for the building HVAC shall be Monday through Friday from 8:00 A.M. to 6:00 P.M., and from 8:00 A.M. – 1:00 P.M. on Saturdays, excluding local, state, and federal holidays (to be defined in the lease).
	Tenant, at tenant's sole cost and expense, shall pay landlord the prevailing after hours HVAC charges in excess of normal building Hours. The current after-hours HVAC charges per the building are sixty-five dollars ($65.00) per hour.
15. Security Deposit:	Landlord shall waive the security deposit.
16. Access:	Building operating hours shall be between 8:00 A.M. and 6:00 P.M., Monday through Friday, and 8:00 A.M.-1:00 P.M. on Saturdays. Please describe afterhours operating costs.

17. Hazardous & Toxic Materials:	Landlord shall have the express responsibility to advise tenant of any toxic materials or hazardous wastes that are located in or about the premises.
18. Americans with Disabilities Act Compliance:	All costs related to compliance with the applicable provisions of the Americans with Disabilities Act of 1990 (ADA) shall be landlord's cost. These costs shall not be a part of any tenant improvement allowance or contribute to increasing operating expenses.
19. Brokerage Commission:	As representatives for Acme Corporation, landlord shall pay Bridge Commercial Properties a commission equal to four percent (4%) of the total lease consideration and any customary leasing bonus due upon lease execution.

This proposal is not legally binding and shall not be construed as an actual lease. Only a fully executed lease agreement shall constitute a lease for the premises, and neither party shall be obligated until both parties have executed said Lease. **This proposal shall remain open until 5:00 p.m., Jan 10, 2011.**

Sincerely,

Scott Johnstone
President
Bridge Commercial Properties
CA Broker # 00950979

AGREED AND ACCEPTED:

Landlord: **Acme Corporation:**

By: _____   By: _____

Title: _____   Title: _____

Date: _____   Date: _____

CALIFORNIA SALE/LEASE AMERICANS WITH DISABILITIES ACT, HAZARDOUS MATERIALS AND TAX DISCLOSURE

The Americans With Disabilities Act is intended to make many business establishments equally accessible to persons with a variety of disabilities. However, modifications to real property may be required. State and local laws also may mandate changes. The real estate brokers in this transaction are not qualified to advise you as to what, if any, changes may be required now, or in the future. Owners and tenants should consult the attorneys and qualified design professionals of their choice for information regarding these matters. Real estate brokers cannot determine which attorneys or design professionals have the appropriate expertise in this area.

Various construction materials may contain items that have been, or may in the future be, determined to be hazardous (toxic) or undesirable and may need to be specifically treated/handled or removed. For example, some transformers and other electrical components contain PCBs, and asbestos has been used in components such as fireproofing, heating, and cooling systems, air duct insulation, spray-on and tile acoustical materials, linoleum, floor tiles, roofing, dry wall, and plaster. Due to prior or current uses of the property or in the area, the property may have hazardous or undesirable metals (including lead based paint), minerals, chemicals, hydrocarbons, or biological hazards (including, but not limited to, mold) or radioactive items (including electrical and magnetic fields) in soil, water, building components, above or below ground containers, or elsewhere in areas that may or may not be accessible or noticeable. Such items may leak or otherwise be released. Real estate agents have no expertise in the detection or correction of hazardous or undesirable items. Expert inspections are necessary. Current or future laws may require clean up by past, present and/or future owners and/or operators. It is the responsibility of the seller/ lessor and buyer/tenant to retain qualified experts to detect and correct such matters and to consult with legal counsel of their choice to determine what provisions, if any, they may include in transaction documents regarding the property.

Sellers/lessors are required under California Health and Safety Code, Section 25915 et seq. to disclose reports and surveys regarding asbestos to certain persons, including their employees, contractors, co-owners, purchasers and tenants. Buyers/ tenants have similar disclosure obligations. Sellers/lessors and buyers/tenants have additional hazardous materials disclosure responsibilities to each other under California Health and Safety Code Section 25359.7 and other California laws. Consult your attorney regarding this matter, and make proper disclosures. Grubb & Ellis Company is not qualified to assist you in this matter or provide you with other legal or tax advice.

Sale, lease and other transactions can have local, state and federal tax consequences for the seller/lessor and/or buyer/ tenant. In the event of a sale, Internal Revenue Cod Section 1445 requires that all buyers of an interest in any real property located in the United States must withhold and pay over to the Internal Revenue Service (IRS) an amount equal to ten percent (10%) of the gross sales price within ten (10) days of the date of the sale unless the buyer can adequately establish that the seller was not a foreigner, generally by having the seller sign a Non-Foreign Seller Certificate. Note that depending upon the structure of the transaction, the tax withholding liability could exceed the net cash proceeds to be paid to the seller at closing. California poses an additional withholding requirement equal to three and one- third percent (3 1/3%) of the gross sales price not only on foreign sellers but also out of state sellers and sellers leaving the state if the sale price exceeds $100,000. Generally, withholding is required if the sales proceeds are distributed outside of California, if the last known address of the seller is outside of California or if a financial intermediary is used. Consult your tax and legal advisor. Real estate brokers are not qualified to give legal or tax advice or to determine whether any other person is properly qualified to provide legal or tax advice.

SELLER/LESSOR   **BUYER/TENANT**

By: _____   By: _____

Title: _____   Title: _____

Date: _____   Date: _____

Property Address: _____

Appendix E: Example Document – Office User – Purchase, Letter of Intent-LOI

Scott W Johnstone
President
Bridge Commercial Properties
4695 MacArthur Court, Ste 1100
Newport Beach, CA 92660

949.555.5555 main
949.555.5555 fax
S@BridgeCommercialProperties.com
www.BridgeCommercialProperties.com

January 1, 2011

John Doe
Any Brokerage Company USA
12345 Any Street, Suite 100
Newport Beach, CA 92660
VIA EMAIL: johndoe@anybroker.com

**Re: Office Condominium Center, Suite 100
     Newport Beach, CA 92660**

Dear Nick,

This Letter of Intent ("Letter") to Purchase represents the basic terms and conditions under which John Smith, ("Buyer") would purchase the property referenced in Paragraph 1 below (the "Property") from Condominium Developer (the "Seller").

1. The Property:	Office Condominium Center is a two story state of the art Office Building. The Property to be sold is approximately 2,000 gross square feet in suite 110 located at 100 Office Condominium Center Drive, Newport Beach, CA.
2. Purchase Price:	The purchase price (the "Purchase Price") shall be One Million Dollars 00/100 Dollars ($1,000,000), which equals $500 per square foot.
3. Deposits/Payment of Purchase Price:	The Purchase Price will be paid as follows:

(a) Upon the opening of Escrow, Buyer will deposit with Escrow Holder the sum of One Hundred Thousand Dollars ($100,000) (the "First Deposit"). Escrow holder shall invest the first deposit in an interest bearing account selected by Buyer with all interest accruing credited to the Purchase Price upon the close of Escrow. The First Deposit shall be invested by Escrow Holder in an interest bearing account selected by Buyer with all interest accruing credited to the Purchase Price upon the close of Escrow. The First Deposit shall become liquidated damages and non-refundable to Buyer and released to Seller upon the expiration of the Inspection Period which shall be thirty (30) days from the opening of escrow. The First Deposit shall be applicable in full towards the Purchase Price.

(b) Upon expiration of the Contingency Period, Buyer will deposit with Escrow Holder the sum of One Hundred Thousand Dollars ($100,000.00) (the "2nd Deposit"). The 2nd Deposit shall be invested by Escrow Holder in an interest bearing account selected by Buyer with all interest accruing credited to the Purchase Price upon the close of Escrow. The 2nd Deposit shall become liquidated damages and non- refundable to Buyer and released to Seller upon its deposit into Escrow. The 2nd Deposit shall be applicable in full towards the Purchase Price.

(c) The balance of the Purchase Price shall be paid through Escrow in cash or by cashiers or certified check upon close of Escrow.

4. Purchase and Sale Agreement:	Seller shall deliver the Agreement to Buyer immediately after mutual execution of this Letter. Buyer and Seller shall enter into an Agreement within **five (5) days** of Buyers receipt of document.
5. Inspection Period:	Seller will afford Buyer reasonable access to the Property in order for Buyer to conduct inspections of a scope satisfactory to Buyer. Buyer shall have a total of **Thirty (30)** days from receipt of Due Diligence materials to conduct its due diligence investigation and waive contingencies. Seller shall make available to the Buyer all documents and records in its possession that are reasonably required for Buyer to conduct its due diligence investigation, including the CC&R's encumbering the project. If Buyer's inspections reveal any condition or information which is not satisfactory to Buyer, to be at Buyer's sole discretion, prior to the expiration of the Inspection Period, Buyer may give written notice to Seller that it elects not to purchase the Property, and the Escrow Company shall return the Deposit, and any interest earned thereon, promptly to Buyer. If Buyer fails to notify Seller that Buyer elects not to purchase the Property by the end of the Inspection Period, then Buyer shall be deemed to have approved the condition of the Property and the Deposit shall become non-refundable and pass through to the Seller.
6. Financing Contingency:	Buyer shall have **Thirty (30)** days from mutual execution of the Agreement to secure a loan commitment for a loan on market terms and conditions reasonably satisfactory to Buyer and waive the Financing Contingency. If Buyer is unable to secure said loan, the Title Company shall return the Deposit, and any interest earned thereon, promptly to Buyer. Upon Seller's request, Buyer shall promptly provide requested information of equity and financing sources to Seller for review and approval.

7. Closing:	The close of escrow shall occur Sixty (60) days after the opening of escrow.
8. Closing Costs:	Each party shall be responsible for its own attorney's fees and other costs associated with due diligence and completing the sale. Each of the parties will pay one-half of the escrow fees. The Buyer shall pay for the cost in excess of the CLTA policy to be provided by the Seller if Buyer desires endorsements or an ALTA policy. Failure to obtain said insurance or other matters required by the Buyer's Lender to close escrow might constitute a default under the terms and conditions of the Agreement.
9. Condition of the Building:	Building shall be delivered in a warm shell condition to include: 1. Finished lobby and hallways 2. Two elevators 3. Two bathrooms on each floor – total of four (4) 4. Electrical room with gears 5. HVAC packages installed on the roof, but not distributed 6. Touch screen electronic directory board
10. As-Is, Where Is:	The property is to be purchased in an "As-Is, Where Is" condition, with no representations or warranties by Seller, express or implied.
11. Pro-rations:	All pro-rations will be as of the Closing Date. Post-Closing reconciliations will be made as described in the Agreement.

12. Agency Disclosure:	In the Agreement, Seller and Buyer will each represent and warrant to the other that it has engaged no broker or intermediary other than Bridge Commercial Properties, which represents the both the Seller and the Buyer, in connection with the proposed transaction and will agree to indemnify the other party for any other loss, liability, and reasonable expenses, including attorneys' fees, incurred by virtue of any action on its part giving rise to a breach of such warranty or a claim for such other fees. Seller will be responsible for commission due to Bridge Commercial Properties pursuant to a separate written agreement.
13. Hazardous Waste/ ADA:	Please refer to the attached Exhibit A, which addresses Federal Law known as the Americans with Disabilities Act and disclosure requirements regarding hazardous waste materials.
14. Confidentiality:	Buyer shall keep confidential all information regarding the Property made available by Seller or Seller's agent(s), except for disclosure to persons assisting Buyer with this transaction and Buyer's lender, if any, and except as may be required by law. This obligation shall survive expiration or termination of this Letter.
15. Commission:	Seller shall pay a commission in accordance with the Exclusive Listing Agreement with Bridge Commercial Properties, which shall be paid through escrow at the close of escrow.

16. Broker Duties:	Buyer hereby acknowledges that they have been and are now advised by the Broker(s) to consult and retain their own experts to advise and represent them concerning the legal and income tax effects of this agreement, as well as the condition and/or legality of the property, the improvements and equipment therein, the soil, thereof, the condition of title thereto, the survey thereof, the environmental aspects thereof, the intended and/or permitted usage thereof, the existence and nature of tenancies therein, any other outstanding agreements, if any, and the existing or contemplated financing thereof and that the Broker(s) is/are not to be responsible for pursuing the investigation of any such matters unless expressly otherwise agreed to in writing by Broker(s) and Buyer or Seller.
17. Dual Agency Disclosure:	In the Agreement, Buyer and Seller will each represent and warrant to the other that it has engaged no broker or intermediary other than Bridge Commercial Properties, which represents both the Buyer and Seller, in connection with the proposed transaction and will agree to indemnify the other party for any other loss, liability, and reasonable expenses, including attorneys' fees, incurred by virtue of any action on its part giving rise to a breach of such warranty or a claim for such other fees. Seller will be responsible for commission due to Bridge Commercial Properties pursuant to a separate written agreement. Both parties are hereby notified of the Dual Agency and agree hereto.

Please evidence your agreement that the foregoing represents an accurate statement of our present mutual intent by signing and returning a copy of this Letter to the undersigned no later than **5:00 PM, January 10, 2010.** In the event this Letter has not been fully executed and returned to the undersigned on or before the above date and time it shall automatically expire and become null and void.

Buyer and Seller acknowledge that this letter does not, and is not intended to, constitute a binding agreement. No party will be otherwise obligated or bound unless and until both parties have entered into the formal purchase agreement. The parties acknowledge that this proposal does not include all of the terms of the purchase agreement.

Respectfully,

Scott W. Johnstone
President
(949) 555-5555
S@BridgeCommercialProperties.com
www.BridgeCommercialProperties.com
License #00950979

AGREED AND ACCEPTED:

Buyer:	**Seller:**
John Smith	Condominium Developer
By: _____	By: _____

Exhibit A

CALIFORNIA SALE/LEASE AMERICANS WITH DISABILITIES ACT, HAZARDOUS MATERIALS, AND TAX DISCLOSURE

The Americans With Disabilities Act is intended to make many business establishments equally accessible to persons with a variety of disabilities; modifications to real property may be required. State and local laws also may mandate changes. The real estate brokers in this transaction are not qualified to advise you as to what, if any, changes may be required now, or in the future.

Owners and tenants should consult attorneys and qualified design professionals of their choice for information regarding these matters. Real estate brokers cannot determine which attorneys or design professionals have the appropriate expertise in this area.

Various construction materials may contain items that have been or may be in the future be determined to be hazardous (toxic) or undesirable and may need to be specifically treated/handled or removed. For example, some transformers and other electrical components contain PCBs, and asbestos has been used in components such as fire-proofing, heating and cooling systems, air duct installation, spray-on and tile acoustical materials, linoleum, floor tiles, roofing, dry wall and plaster. Due to prior uses of the Property or in the area, the Property may have hazardous or undesirable metals (including lead-based paint), minerals, chemicals, hydrocarbons, or biological hazards (including, but not limited to, mold) or radioactive items (including electrical and magnetic fields) in soils, water building components, above or below-ground containers or elsewhere in areas that may or may not be accessible or noticeable. Such items may leak or otherwise be elsewhere in areas that may or may not be accessible or noticeable. Such items may leak or otherwise be released. Real estate agents have no expertise in the detection or correction or hazardous or undesirable items. Expert inspections are necessary. Current or future laws may require clean up by pas, present and/ or future owners and/or operators. It is the responsibility of the Seller/Lessor and the Buyer/Tenant to retain qualified experts to detect and correct such maters and to consult with legal counsel of their choice to determine what provisions, if any, they may include in transaction documents regarding the Property.

Sellers/Lessors are required under California Health and Safety Code Section 25915 et seq., to disclose reports and surveys regarding asbestos to certain persons, including their employees, contractors, co-owners, purchasers and tenants. Buyers/Tenants have similar disclosure obligations. Sellers/Lessors and Buyers/Tenants have additional hazardous materials disclosure responsibilities to each other under California Health and safety Code Section 25359.7 and other California laws. Consult your attorney regarding this matter, and make proper disclosures. Grubb & Ellis Company is not qualified to assist you in this matter or provide you with other legal or tax advice.

Sale, lease and other transactions can have local, state and federal tax consequences for the seller/lessor and/or buyer/tenant. In the event of a sale, Internal Revenue Cod Section 1445 requires that all buyers of an interest in any real property located in the United States must withhold and pay over to the Internal Revenue Service (IRS) an amount equal to ten percent (10%) of the gross sales price within ten (10) days of the date of the sale unless the buyer can adequately establish that the seller was not a foreigner, generally by having the seller sign a Non-Foreign Seller Certificate. Note that depending upon the structure of the transaction, the tax withholding liability could exceed the net cash proceeds to be paid to the seller at closing. California poses an additional withholding requirement equal to three and one-third percent (3 1/3%) of the gross sales price not only on foreign sellers but also out of state sellers and sellers leaving the state if the sale price exceeds $100,000. Generally, withholding is required if the sales proceeds are distributed outside of California, if the last known address of the seller is outside of California or if a financial intermediary is used. Consult your tax and legal advisor. Real estate brokers are not qualified to give legal or tax advice or to determine whether any other person is properly qualified to provide legal or tax advice.

SELLER/LESSOR   **BUYER/TENANT**

By: _____   By: _____

Title: _____   Title: _____

Date: _____   Date: _____

Appendix F: Example Document – Office Investor – Purchase, Letter of Intent-LOI

January 1, 2011

Mr. Scott Johnstone
Bridge Commercial Properties
4695 MacArthur Court, Suite 1000
Newport Beach, CA 92660

John Doe
Principle
Acme CRE Investment Company Inc
111 First St, Suite 100
Newport Beach, CA 926660

949.555.5555 main
949.555.5555 fax
CA License # 00950979

**Re: Purchase Offer,
Letter of Intent
1111 Pacific Coast Highway
Newport Beach, CA 92660**

Dear Scott:

This letter summarizes the basic business terms and conditions upon which Acme CRE Investment Company Inc, or its assignee, ("Buyer") would purchase the property located at 1111 Pacific Coast Highway, Newport Beach, CA 92660 APN 123-456-789, containing approximately 150,000 square feet of land and (1) improvement thereon, including the approximately 40,000 square foot, two-story office building and associated surface parking lot. There shall be parking spaces providing a 4/1,000 square feet ratio of dedicated parking spaces; (2) all construction and other warranties associated with the property; (3) all personal property located at or used in connection with the operation and management of such property; and (4) all appurtenances, licenses, permits, contracts and intangible property affecting the property (collectively, "Property") from the current owner ABC Development Company ("Seller").

1. **Property Description:**	The property is described as a 40,000 SF Two Story Office building located at 1111 Pacific Coast Highway, Newport Beach, CA 92660 APN # 123-456-789.
2. **Purchase Price:**	The purchase price ("Purchase Price") for the Property shall be Twenty Million Dollars ($20,000,000) payable as follows:

A. Buyer shall deposit the sum of One-Hundred-and-Fifty-Thousand Dollars ($150,000) ("Initial Deposit") with First American Title Company ("Escrow Holder") concurrently with the execution of a definitive Purchase and Sale Agreement and Joint Escrow Instructions ("PSA"). Upon the satisfactory approval by Buyer of the "Due Diligence Materials" (defined below), Buyer shall increase the Initial Deposit by One-Hundred- and-Fifty-Thousand Dollars ($150,000) ("Additional Deposit".) (The Initial Deposit and the Additional Deposit will be collectively referred to as, the "Deposit"). The Deposit shall become non-refundable upon Buyer's removal or waiver of its contingencies as set forth in the PSA, subject to satisfaction of any remaining conditions to the closing. Escrow Holder shall invest the Initial Deposit and the Additional Deposit in an interest-bearing account or other investment instrument designated by Buyer, with interest accruing and payable to Buyer.

B. The balance of the Purchase Price shall be Nineteen-Million-Seven-Hundred Thousand Dollars ($19,700,000) shall be paid in cash upon closing through Escrow.

3. Escrow:	A. Upon execution of the PSA, which Buyer will prepare in a timely manner, and escrow ("Escrow") shall be opened with First American ("Escrow Holder"), and Buyer and Seller agree to execute such additional escrow instructions as Escrow Holder deems reasonably necessary or advisable in order to effect the terms of the PSA. The opening of Escrow shall be deemed to be the date upon which Buyer and Seller deliver executed counterparts of the PSA to Escrow Holder.
	B. Escrow shall close and the Grant Deed recorded ("Closing") on the date that is Forty-Five (45) days after the Contingency Date.
4. Contingencies:	A. Buyer's obligation to purchase the Property shall be conditioned upon satisfaction of each of the contingencies set forth in the PSA on or before the date ("Contingency Date") that is Thirty (30) days after the later of (a) execution of the PSA or (b) delivery to Buyer of the last of the Due Diligence Materials set forth in the PSA, such items to include, but not limited to, the items set forth on Exhibit A attached to this.

In the event that Buyer does not affirmatively approve of the Due Diligence Materials on or before the Contingency Date, Then the PSA shall automatically terminate, and Escrow Holder shall return the Deposit (and all accrued interest thereon) immediately to Buyer:

> B. During the period ending on the Contingency Date ("Contingency Period"),Buyer shall have the right to inspect and approve (i) all physical, mechanical, structural, seismic and all other aspects of the Property, (ii) each of the Due Diligence Materials and (iii) all books, records and files regarding the Property, and to make inquiries and investigations as Buyer deems necessary or appropriate.

Seller will cause its consultants to furnish Buyer with any information and copies of documents reasonably requested by Buyer during the Contingency Period. In addition, the Buyer shall have the right to enter The Property to interview the property manager and tenants and to conduct reasonable tests and inspections deemed reasonably necessary or advisable by Buyer or its consultants including, but not limited to, physical inspection, calculations of floor areas and inspections of the improvements;

C. Seller shall maintain the Property in good condition and repair and shall maintain adequate casualty liability insurance covering the Property until the Closing. Seller shall not enter into any lease, contract or other agreement affecting the Property, or amend or terminate any of the same, without Buyer's approval, which shall not be unreasonably withheld or delayed;

D. The PSA shall contain standard terms and conditions that are typically found in an acquisition of this size and nature, including, but not limited to, title, buyer: 12345 Big City Drive, Suite 1000, Los Angeles, CA 90000 | (310) 555-5555 t | (310) 555-5555 f

Seller representations and warranties, pro-rations, assignments of tenant leases and marketing of the property post acceptance of this letter;

E. All of Seller's and Buyer's covenants required to have been performed by the Closing shall have been so performed, and all representations and warranties of each of Seller and Buyer shall be current as of the Closing and no material changes in the physical of financial condition of the property shall have occurred as of the Closing

	Approval of the foregoing conditions shall be in writing signed by Buyer. Failure of Buyer to approve any Due Diligence Materials on or before the Contingency Date (or such other date which may be expressly specified above) conclusively shall be deemed to constitute Buyer's disapproval thereof, and the Deposit (and all accrued interest thereon) shall be returned to Buyer (and the Deposit shall also be returned to Buyer if Buyer's closing conditions are not satisfied); F. Financing Contingency: None G. Estoppel Certificates. Buyer's obligations shall be further conditioned upon obtaining "clean" estoppels certificates (in a form reasonably acceptable to Buyer) from Seventy-Five (75%) percent of all the tenants and all of the major tenants.
5. Brokerage Commissions; Closing Expenses:	Each of Buyer and Seller shall pay for and indemnify the other against any brokerage commission or transaction fee owed as a result of the engagement by Buyer or Seller of a broker or other person in connection with this transaction, except that Seller shall pay a brokerage fee to Scott Johnstone of Bridge Commercial Properties. ("Broker"), as agreed to by Seller and Broker in a separate agreement. Buyer and Seller shall each bear their own legal fees, and all escrow fees, title and recording charges, conveyance taxes and all other closing expenses shall be borne or charged in accordance with customs of the Orange County market.
6. Marketing:	Seller is prohibited from marketing, soliciting or accepting any offers from prospective buyers during the Contingency Period, or anytime thereafter if Buyer waives contingencies and approves of the Due Diligence Materials. Additionally, Seller shall not, without Buyer's prior written approval, enter into, amend or terminate any leases or contracts affecting the Property or take any other actions affecting the Property from the date of acceptance hereof through the earlier of (a) the Closing or (b) the termination of the Purchase Agreement. Notwithstanding the foregoing, Buyer will have the right to market the Property for lease during this period.

7. Terms of Offer/Non-Binding Affect:	The foregoing offer may be accepted by Seller by executing and returning a counterpart of this letter to Buyer on or before 5:00 p.m. on January 10, 2011.
	Upon acceptance, Buyer shall cause the PSA to be prepared, incorporating the terms of this letter, together with such other customary terms and provisions and representations and warranties applicable to a transaction of this nature. This letter shall not constitute a formal and binding agreement and shall not create any legal rights or obligations between parties. It is intended that all legal rights and obligations between parties be created under and governed solely by the PSA when the same is fully executed by Buyer and Seller. Notwithstanding the foregoing, during the course of negotiation of the PSA, Seller agrees not to market the Property to other parties, nor to solicit offers for the acquisitions of the Property.

We look forward to working with you toward consummating this transaction.

Very truly yours,

John Doe
Principle
Acme CRE Investment Company Inc.

AGREED AND ACCEPTED:

Buyer: **Seller:**

John Doe, Acme CRE Investment   ABC Development Company
Company Inc.

By: _____   By: _____

EXHIBIT A

DUE DILIGENCE MATERIALS

Buyer shall have had the opportunity to review and approve, at a minimum, each of the following:

(1) A copy of a current rent roll describing the occupancy status of the Property as of the beginning of the current month as well as monthly rent rolls for each of the previous twenty four (24) calendar months;

(2) A copy of the bank statements for the property for the prior twenty four(24) months that reflect deposits that reconcile with rent amounts reflected on the rent rolls provided;

(3) A current preliminary title report including the legal description of the Property, together with copies of all documents referred to therein, prepared by a First American ("Title Company");

(4) Evidence that the Property complies with all applicable codes and The Subdivision requirements;

(5) A current ALTA Survey of the Property;

(6) A copy of the leases or rental agreements for tenants of the Property and any amendments and letter agreements relating thereto including any license agreements and current financial statements on the tenant(s);

(7) Copies of all licenses, service contracts (including parking, elevator, HVAC and landscaping maintenance contracts), management contracts, brokerage agreements, permits, variances, insurance policies, maps, association or property owner agreements, certificates of occupancy, building permits and other documentation and evidence that the construction, present use, occupancy and operation of the Property is authorized by and is in compliance with all governmental regulations; certificates of occupancy and similar type occupancy approval documents;

(8) Warranties (e.g., for vertical transportation, HVAC and other building systems);

(9) Projected or actual Operating statements of the Property for calendar year 2007, 2008, 2009 and 2010 monthly statements to date;

(10) Allplans,structuraldrawings,architecturaland"asbuilt"drawings,including, but not limited to, mechanical, electrical, air conditioning, landscape and sprinkler drawings and specifications regarding the improvements, and

any soils, structural, geological, environmental, hazardous materials and asbestos studies or reports relating to subsurface conditions, grading plans, topographical maps arid similar data respecting the Property;

(11) Copies of property tax bills for the last three (3) years and copies of the most recently available utility bills and similar records respecting the Property;

(12) A list of all personal property owned by or leased by Seller and used in connection with the ownership or operation of the Property;

(13) A certificate of Seller certifying to Seller's knowledge that there is no legal or administrative action, proceeding, claim, arbitration or suit pending before any court, agency or official, nor any such claim or action threatened in writing, relating to the Seller, the Property or with respect to the validity of any statutes, ordinances, regulations or restrictions or any permits or approvals thereunder relating to the Property, nor any outstanding contingent liabilities affecting the Property;

(14) To the best of Seller's knowledge, a detailed written description of the status of current tenant occupancies and future plans including any and all proposals, agreements and correspondence outstanding with any prospective tenants;

(15) All available historical environmental reports, Phase I's and/or Phase II's;

(16) Copies of any reports (such as physical, seismic, environmental or other such reports), surveys or other information on any Matters that Seller may have received as part of the current sales process for the Property; and

(17) Such other matters as agreed to in the Purchase and Sale Agreement.

Appendix G: Example Document – Deal Process Timeline and Flowchart

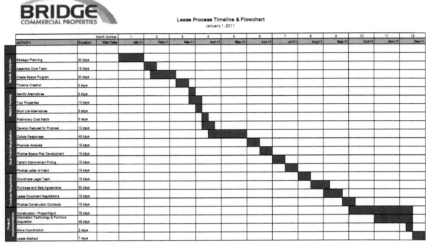

Appendix H: Example Document – Capabilities Brochure – Tenant

BRIDGE
COMMERCIAL PROPERTIES

Scott W Johnstone
President
949.555.5555 office / 949.555.5555 cell
scott@bridgecre.com
CA Broker #00950979

- 25 Years of Experience
- Specializing in Office Properties
- Tenant Representation

Hana Paradeiser
Marketing Coordinator
949.555.5555 office / 818.555.5555 cell
h@bridgecre.com

- 10 Years of Marketing Experience

Team Experience

Our Team has over **25 years** of combined experience and has been responsible for over $3 billion in real estate transactions throughout our award-winning careers.

Team Capabilities

The combination of a sole proprietors mentality and attention to detail mixed with institutional experience truly makes us the best single source solution for all of your Corporate Real Estate needs.

- Lease Renegotiation
- Multimarket Corporate Representation
- Property Analysis + Space Optimization
- Architectural Review
- Relocation Analysis
- Site Acquisition

- Employee Location Optimization
- Construction Management
- Lease Administration
- Market Data & Analysis
- Property Analysis
- Lease Negotiations

Deal Announcement:

Bridge Commercial Properties this week successfully represented Acme Widgit Corporation in the relocation of their corporate headquarters to the 1234 Professional Center Drive, Newport Beach, California. The ten year lease transaction takes Acme Widgit Corporation's offices to 20,000 square feet and allows for their continued leadership role and growth in the widgit marketplace. The lease saved Acme Widgit Corporation nearly $5,000,000 in rent over the term of their lease. Thank you *Acme Widgit Corporation* for your continued support. January 1, 2011

ACME WIDGIT
CORPORATION

CALL US TODAY FOR MORE INFORMATION REGARDING OUR CONSULTATIVE APPROCH TO COMMERCIAL REAL ESTATE SERVICES

Whether you are looking to renegotiate or renew your lease, relocate, expand or contract your office, our team is ready and committed to helping you make smarter, faster decisions, while maximizing market leverage, reducing your costs and freeing your valuable time.

Appendix I: Example Document – Market Newsletter

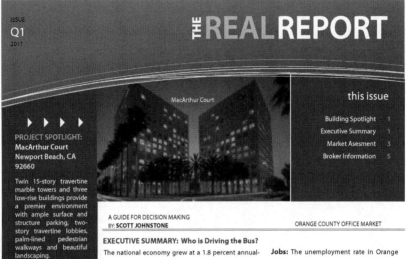

ISSUE
Q1
2011

THE REAL REPORT

MacArthur Court

this issue

▶ ▶ ▶ ▶

PROJECT SPOTLIGHT:
MacArthur Court
Newport Beach, CA
92660

Twin 15-story travertine marble towers and three low-rise buildings provide a premier environment with ample surface and structure parking, two-story travertine lobbies, palm-lined pedestrian walkways and beautiful landscaping.

Five buildings totaling 690,000 sq/ft

Easy access to the 405 and 55 Freeways and 73 Toll Road

Ample surface and structure parking

Seconds to John Wayne Airport

On-site café and banks with ATM

On-site convenience store and auto detailing

Rental Rates:

$1.95 - $2.45 FSG

A GUIDE FOR DECISION MAKING
BY: **SCOTT JOHNSTONE**   ORANGE COUNTY OFFICE MARKET

EXECUTIVE SUMMARY: Who is Driving the Bus?

The national economy grew at a 1.8 percent annualized rate in the first quarter according to the advance estimate of gross domestic product from the Bureau of Economic Analysis. Consumer spending made the biggest contribution, adding 1.9 percentage points, although this was below the 2.8-point contribution made by consumers in the fourth quarter. Inventory additions and business spending on equipment and software also contributed to growth. Late last year, many economists raised their GDP forecasts in response to the $858 billion package of tax cut extensions and new tax cuts passed by Congress in December. But recently many have lowered their forecasts due to rising energy prices and the uncertain outlook for the Middle East, Japan and the Europe. The Employment Situation report, which the Bureau of Labor Statistics will release Friday, May 6, will be even more important than usual because it will reveal whether the drags on economic growth are affecting the labor market, which is a major driver of demand for commercial real estate.

Jobs: The unemployment rate in Orange County was 8.9% in February 2011 and below the year-ago estimate of 9.7%. This compares with an unadjusted unemployment rate of 12.3% for California and 9.5% for the nation during the same time period. According to the State of California Employment Development Department, Orange County increased overall by 16,300 payroll jobs from February 2010 to February 2011; the largest gains were 6,500 in leisure and hospitality and 5,400 in professional & business services. However, during that same period, Orange County lost 2,000 jobs in trade, transportation, and utilities. Chapman University is forecasting that 23,000 jobs will be added in Orange County in 2011.

BRIDGE
COMMERCIAL PROPERTIES

The Next Shoe to Drop: The dollar volume of direct investment in commercial properties soared by 77 percent in the first quarter of 2011 compared with the first quarter of 2010. Last year, the market was depicted by a barbell with investors focusing on core properties in primary, supply constrained markets at one end, and distressed assets priced for a quick sale at the other end. Attracted by higher yields, investors now are taking a fresh look at properties in secondary markets and properties below the trophy threshold. Source: Real Capital Analytics

• Outstanding levels of distressed assets were essentially flat in the first quarter compared with the fourth quarter of 2010 on the heels of a 4 percent decline between the third and fourth quarters of last year. This suggests that the level of distress may be topping out. Source: Real Capital Analytics

• First quarter returns for direct property ownership totaled 3.36 percent, the fourth consecutive quarterly increase of the current recovery cycle. The return included two components: 1.52 percent from income and 1.84 percent from appreciation. Source: NCREIF

• Publicly traded REITs returned 6.8 percent in the first quarter, beating the 5.4 percent return posted by the S&P 500. Sources: NAREIT, Bloomberg

This is a pretty good performance for an asset class that, 24 months ago, was called "the next shoe to drop."

Big Picture: The Orange County office maket continued to convey signs of recovery in the first quarter of 2011. Both vacancy and availability decreased from the previous quarter, and net absorption displayed positive numbers for three consecurive quarters, producing a total of over 1.23 million square feet of positive absorption since the third quarter of 2010. Demand, though, still weak by historical standards, picked of a renewed interest in states transactions. While these are positive indications, stability will need to be sustained in coming quarters to be considered recovery.

Summary: We are beginning to see a decrease in the amount of available space being added per quarter, as well as an overall increase in investment sales activity. As we enter into 2011, positive absorption continues, and with few new deliveries in the pipeline to apply upward pressure on vacancy, the market has begun to stabilize. We forsee a continued increase in investment activity in the coming quarters as lenders dispose of distressed assets. Lease rates are expected to remain soft for the near future, and concessions in the forms of free rent, reduced parking fees, relocation funds and tenant improvement allowances should continue in order to incentivize tenants to act immediately. We should also see an increase in leasing activity as many short-term deals come up for renewal. As job creation continues and consumer confidence stabilizes, the office market will continue to recover.

Notable Market Transactions:

20532 El Toro Road - Sale	35 Tesla - Sale	3200 Park Center Dr. - Lease
Mission Viejo	Laguna Hills	Costa Mesa
Buyer: **JP Morgan Chase**	Buyer: **Owen Commercial**	Tenant: **Hyundai**
Size: 52,091 Square Feet	Size: 36,000 Square Feet	Size: 147,712 Square Feet

Orange County

First Quarter 2011 Office Market Trends

Vacant Space by Submarket

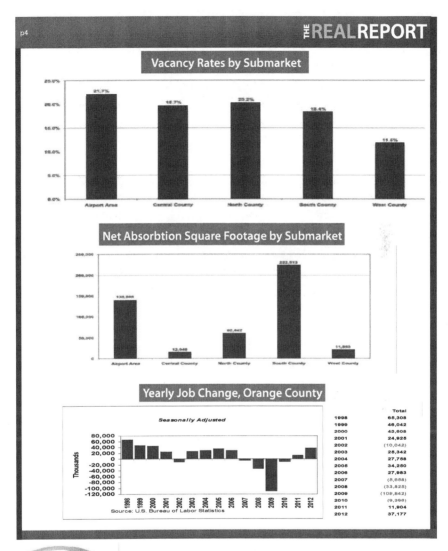

p5

ᵀᴴᴱ REAL REPORT

More Notable Market Transactions:

275 Valencia Ave

Brea - Lease

Tenant: **Bank of America**

Size: 637,000 Square Feet

18101 Von Karman Ave.

Irvine - Lease

Tenant: **Epicor Software**

Size: 68,235 Square Feet

1310 Old Ranch Parkway

Seal Beach - Sale

Buyer: **AIG Global**

Size: 280,6113 Square Feet

TEAM EXPERIENCE

Our Team has over **25 years** of combined experience and has been responsible for over $3 billion in real estate transactions throughout our award-winning careers.

The combination of a sole proprietors mentality and attention to detail mixed with institutional experience truly makes us the best single source solution for all of your Corporate Real Estate needs.

TEAM CAPABILITIES

- Lease Renegotiation
- Multimarket Corporate Representation
- Property Analysis + Space Optimization
- Architectural Review
- Relocation Analysis
- Site Aquisition
- Employee Location Optimization
- Construction Management
- Lease Administration
- Market Data & Analysis
- Property Analysis
- Lease Negotiations

Deal Announcement:

Bridge Commercial Properties this week successfully represented Acme Widgit Corporation in the relocation of their corporate headquarters to the 1234 Professional Center Drive, Newport Beach, California. The ten year lease transaction takes Acme Widgit Corporation's offices to 20,000 square feet and allows for their continued leadership role and growth in the widgit marketplace. The lease saved Acme Widgit Corporation nearly $5,000,000 in rent over the term of their lease. Thank you *Acme Widgit Corporation* for your continued support. January 1, 2011

ACME WIDGIT CORPORATION

SCOTT JOHNSTONE
President
Bridge Commercial Properties
CA License # 00950979

P 949.555.5555
C 949.555.5555

s@bridgecre.com

HANA PARADEISER
Marketing Coordinator
Bridge Commercial Properties

P 949.555.5555
C 818.555.5555

h@bridgecre.com

BRIDGE
COMMERCIAL PROPERTIES

Glossary: Industry Terminology

Abatement: Often and commonly referred to as *free rent* or *early occupancy* and may occur outside or in addition to the primary term of the lease.

Above Building Standard: Upgraded finishes and specialized designs necessary to accommodate a tenant's requirements.

Absorption: The rate, expressed as a percentage, at which available space in the marketplace is leased during a predetermined period. Also referred to as "Market Absorption"

Absorption Rate: The net change in space available for lease between two dates, typically expressed as a percentage of the total square footage.

Ad Valorem: According to value. This is a tax imposed on the value of property (references a general property tax), which is typically based on the local government's valuation of the property.

Add-On Factor: Often referred to as the Loss Factor or Rentable/ Usable (R/U) Factor, it represents the tenant's pro-rata share of the Building Common Areas, such as lobbies, public corridors, and restrooms. It's usually expressed as a percentage, which can then be applied to the usable square footage to determine the rentable square footage upon which the tenant will pay rent.

Allowance Over Building Shell: Most often used in a yet-to-be constructed property, the tenant has a blank canvas upon which to customize the interior finishes to their specifications. This arrangement caps the landlord's expenditure at a fixed dollar amount over the negotiated price of the base building shell. This arrangement is most successful when both parties agree on a detailed definition of what construction is included and at what price.

Anchor Tenant: The major or prime tenant in a shopping center, building, etc.

Annual Percentage Rate (APR): The actual cost of borrowing money, expressed in the form of an annual interest rate. It may be higher than the note rate because it represents full disclosure of the interest rate, loan origination fees, loan discount points, and other credit costs paid to the lender.

Appraisal: An estimate of opinion and value based upon a factual analysis of a property by a qualified professional.

Appreciation: The increased value of an asset.

"As-Is" Condition: The acceptance by the tenant of the existing condition of the premises at the time the lease is consummated. This would include any physical defects.

Assessment: A fee imposed on property, usually to pay for public improvements such as water, sewers, streets, improvement districts, etc.

Assignment: A transfer by lessee of lessee's entire estate in the property. Distinguishable from a sublease where the sublessee acquires something less than the lessee's entire interest.

Attorn: To turn over or transfer to another money or goods. To agree to recognize a new owner of a property and to pay him/her rent. In a lease, when the tenant agrees to attorn to the purchaser, the landlord is given the power to subordinate tenant's interest to any first mortgage or deed of trust lien subsequently placed upon the leased premises.

Balloon Payment: A large principal payment that typically becomes due at the conclusion of the loan term. Generally, it reflects a loan amortized over a longer period than that of the term of the loan itself (i.e. payments based on a 25-year amortization with the principal balance due at the end of 5 years). See "Bullet Loan."

Bankrupt: The condition or state of a person (individual, partnership, corporation, etc.) who are unable to repay its debts as they are, or become, due.

Bankruptcy: Proceedings under federal statures to relieve a debtor who is unable or unwilling to pay its debts. After addressing certain priorities and exemptions, the bankrupt's property and other assets are distributed by the court to creditors as full satisfaction for the debt. See also: "Chapter 11."

Base Rent: A set amount used as a minimum rent in a lease with provisions for increasing the rent over the term of the lease. See also "Escalation Clause," "Operating Expense Escalation" and "Percentage Lease."

Base Year: Actual taxes and operating expenses for a specified base year, most often the year in which the lease commences. Once the base year expenses are known, the lease essentially becomes a dollar stop lease.

Below-Grade: Any structure or a portion of a structure located underground or below the surface grade of the surrounding land.

Building Classifications: Building classifications in most markets refer to Class "A," "B," "C" and sometimes "D" properties. While the rating assigned to a particular building is very subjective, Class "A" properties are typically newer buildings with superior construction and finish in excellent locations with easy access, attractive to credit tenants, and which offer a multitude of amenities such as on-site management or covered parking. These buildings, of course, command the highest rental rates in their sub-market. As the "Class" of the building decreases (i.e. Class "B," "C" or "D") one component or another such as age, location or construction of the building becomes less desirable. Note that a Class "A" building in one sub-market might rank lower if it were located in a distinctly different sub-market just a few miles away containing a higher end product.

Building Code: The various laws set forth by the ruling municipality as to the end use of a certain piece of property and that dictate the criteria for design, materials, and type of improvements allowed.

Building Load or "Core" Factor: Represents the percentage of Net Rentable Square Feet devoted to the building's common areas (lobbies, rest rooms, corridors, etc.). This factor can be computed for an entire building or a single floor of a building. Also known as a Loss Factor or Rentable/Usable (R/U) Factor, it's calculated by dividing the rentable square footage by the usable square footage. See also "Rentable/Usable Ratio."

Building Standard: A list of construction materials and finishes that represent what the Tenant Improvement (Finish) Allowance/ Work Letter is designed to cover while also serving to establish the landlord's minimum quality standards with respect to tenant finish improvements within the building. Examples of standard building items are: type and style of doors, lineal feet of partitions, quantity of lights, quality of floor covering, etc.

Building Standard Plus Allowance: The landlord lists, in detail, the building standard materials and costs necessary to make the premises suitable for occupancy. A negotiated allowance is then provided for the tenant to customize or upgrade materials. See also "Work Letter."

Build-Out: The space improvements put in place per the tenant's specifications. Takes into consideration the amount of Tenant Finish Allowance provided for in the lease agreement. See also "Tenant Improvement Allowance"

Build-To-Suit: An approach taken to lease space by a property owner where a new building is designed and constructed per the tenant's specifications.

: This type of expense is most often defined by reference to generally accepted **Bullet Loan:** Any short-term, generally five to seven years, financing option that requires a balloon payment at the end of the term and anticipates that the loan will be refinanced in order to meet the **Balloon Payment** obligation. Essentially, should the refinancing not be available, often due to the property not performing as anticipated, the borrower is "shot" and the property is subject to foreclosure. An example of this is when a developer borrows to cover the costs of construction and carry-costs for a new building with the expectation that it would be replaced by long-term (or "permanent") financing provided by an institutional investor once most of risk involved in construction and lease-up had been overcome resulting in an income-producing property.

Capital Expenses: accounting principles (GAAP), but GAAP does not provide definitive guidance on all possible expenditures. Accountants will often disagree on whether or not to include certain items.

Capitalization: A method of determining value of real property by considering net operating income divided by a predetermined annual rate of return. See "Capitalization Rate."

Capitalization Rate: The rate that is considered a reasonable return on investment (based on both the investor's alternative investment possibilities and the risk of the investment). Used to determine and value real property through the capitalization process. Also called "free and clear return." See "Capitalization."

Carrying Charges: Costs incidental to property ownership, other than interest (i.e. taxes, insurance costs and maintenance expenses), that must be absorbed by the landlord during the initial lease-up of a building and thereafter during periods of vacancy.

Certificate of Occupancy: A document presented by a local government agency or building department certifying that a building and/or the leased premises (tenant's space), has been satisfactorily inspected, and is/are in a condition suitable for occupancy.

Chapter 7: That portion of the Federal Bankruptcy code that deals with business liquidations. Chapter 11 is that part of the Federal Bankruptcy code that deals with business reorganizations.

Chapter 11: That portion of the Federal Bankruptcy code that deals with business reorganizations. Chapter 7 is that part of the Federal Bankruptcy code that deals with business liquidations.

Clear-Span Facility: A building, most often a warehouse or parking garage, with vertical columns on the outside edges of the structure and a clear span between columns.

Circulation Factor: Interior space required for internal office circulation not accounted for in the Net Square Footage. Based upon our experience, we use a Circulation Factor of 1.35 x the Net Square Footage for office and fixed drywall areas and a Circulation Factor of 1.45 x the Net Square Footage for open area workstations. See also "Net Square Footage and "Usable Square Footage.

Common Area: There are two components of the term "common area." If referred to in association with the Rentable/Usable or Load Factor calculation, the common areas are those areas within a building that are available for common use by all tenants or groups of tenants and their invitees (i.e. lobbies, corridors, restrooms, etc.). On the other hand, the cost of maintaining parking facilities, malls, sidewalks, landscaped areas, public toilets, truck and service facilities, and the like are included in the term "common area" when calculating the tenant's pro-rata share of building operating expenses.

Common Area Maintenance (CAM): This is the amount of Additional Rent charged to the tenant, in addition to the Base Rent, to maintain the common areas of the property shared by the tenants and from which all tenants benefit. Examples include: snow removal, outdoor lighting, parking lot sweeping, insurance, property taxes, etc. Most often, this does not include any capital improvements see "Capital Expenses" that are made to the property.

Comparables: Lease rates and terms of properties similar in size, construction quality, age, use, and typically located within the same sub-market and used as comparison properties to determine the fair market lease rate for another property with similar characteristics.

Concessions: Cash or cash equivalents expended by the landlord in the form of rental abatement, additional tenant finish allowance, moving expenses, cabling expenses or other monies expended to influence or persuade the tenant to sign a lease.

Condemnation: The process of taking private property, without the consent of the owner, by a governmental agency for public use through the power of eminent domain. See also "Eminent Domain."

Construction Management: The actual construction process is overseen by a qualified construction manager who ensures that the various stages of the construction process are completed in a timely and seamless fashion, from getting the construction permit to completion of the construction to the final walk-through of the completed leased premises with the tenant.

Consumer Price Index ("CPI"): Measures inflation in relation to the change in the price of a fixed market basket of goods and services purchased by a specified population during a "base" period. It's not a true "cost of living" factor and bears little direct relation to actual costs of building operation or the value of real estate. The CPI is commonly used to increase the base rental periodically as a means of protecting the landlord's rental stream against inflation or to provide a cushion for operating expense increases for a landlord unwilling to undertake the record keeping necessary for operating expense escalations.

Contiguous Space: (1) Multiple suites/spaces within the same building and on the same floor, which can be combined and rented to a single tenant. (2) A block of space located on multiple adjoining floors in a building (i.e., a tenant leases floors 6 through 12 in a building).

Contract Documents: The complete set of design plans and specifications for the construction of a building or of a building's interior improvements. Working Drawings specify for the contractor the precise manner in which a project is to be constructed. See also "Specifications" and "Working Drawings."

Conveyance: Most commonly refers to the transfer of title to property between parties by deed. The term may also include most of the instruments by which an interest in real estate is created, mortgaged, or assigned.

Core Factor: Represents the percentage of Net Rentable Square Feet devoted to the building's common areas (lobbies, rest rooms, corridors, etc.). This factor can be computed for an entire building or a single floor of a building. Also known as a Loss Factor or Rentable/ Usable (R/U) Factor, it's calculated by dividing the rentable square footage by the usable square footage."

Cost Approach: A method of appraising real property whereby the replacement cost of a structure is calculated using current costs of construction.

Covenant: A written agreement inserted into deeds or other legal instruments stipulating performance or non-performance of certain acts or, uses or non-use of a property and/or land.

Covenant of Quiet Enjoyment: The old "quiet enjoyment" paragraph, now more commonly referred to as "Warranty of Possession," had nothing to do with noise in and around the leased premises. It provides a warranty by landlord that it has the legal ability to convey the possession of the premises to tenant; the landlord does not warrant that he owns the land. This is the essence of the landlord's agreement and the tenant's obligation to pay rent. This means that if the landlord breaches this warranty, it constitutes an actual or constructive eviction.

Cumulative Discount Rate: The interest rate used in finding present values that when applied to the rental rate takes into account all landlord lease concessions and then expressed as a percentage of base rent.

Dedicate: To appropriate private property to public ownership for a public use.

Deed: A legal instrument transferring title to real property from the seller to the buyer upon the sale of such property.

Deed in Lieu of Foreclosure: A deed given by an owner/borrower to a lender to satisfy a mortgage debt and avoid foreclosure. See also "Foreclosure."

Deed of Trust: An instrument used in many states in place of a mortgage by which real property is transferred to a trustee by the borrower (trustor), in favor of the lender (beneficiary), to secure repayment of a debt.

Default: The general failure to perform a legal or contractual duty or to discharge an obligation when due. Some specific examples are: 1) Failure to make a payment of rent when due. 2) The breach or failure to perform any of the terms of a lease agreement.

Deficiency Judgment: Imposition of personal liability on a borrower for the unpaid balance of mortgage debt after a foreclosure has failed to yield the full amount of the debt.

Demising Walls: The partition wall that separates one tenant's space from another or from the building's common area such as a public corridor.

Design/Build: A system in which a single entity is responsible for both the design and construction. The term can apply to an entire facility or to individual components of the construction to be performed by a subcontractor; also referred to as "design/construct."

Depreciation: Spreading out the cost of a capital asset over its estimated useful life or a decrease in the usefulness, and therefore value, of real property improvements or other assets caused by deterioration or obsolescence.

Distraint: The act of seizing (legally or illegally) personal property based on the right and interest that a landlord has in the property of a tenant in default.

Dollar Stop: An agreed dollar amount of taxes and operating expense (expressed for the building as a whole or on a square foot basis) over which the tenant will pay its prorated share of increases. May be applied to specific expenses (e.g., property taxes or insurance). Otherwise known as an "Expense Stop."

Earnest Money: The monetary advance by a buyer of part of the purchase price to indicate the intention and ability of the buyer to carry out the contract.

Easement: A right of use over the property of another created by grant, reservation, agreement, prescription or necessary implication. It's either for the benefit of adjoining land ("appurtenant"), such as the right to cross A to get to B., or for the benefit of a specific individual ("in gross"), such as a public utility easement.

Economic Feasibility: A building or project's feasibility in terms of costs and revenue, with excess revenue establishing the degree of viability.

Economic Rent: The market rental value of a property at a given point in time, even though the actual rent may be different.

Effective Rent: The actual rental rate to be achieved by the landlord after deducting the value of concessions from the base rental rate paid by a tenant, usually expressed as an average rate over the term of the lease.

Efficiency Factor: Represents the percentage of Net Rentable Square Feet devoted to the building's common areas (lobbies, rest rooms, corridors, etc.). This factor can be computed for an entire building or a single floor of a building. Also known as a Core Factor or Rentable/Usable (R/U) Factor, it's calculated by dividing the rentable square footage by the usable square footage.

Eminent Domain: A power of the state, municipalities, and private persons or corporations authorized to exercise functions of public character to acquire private property for public use by condemnation, in return for just compensation. See also "Condemnation."

Encroachment: The intrusion of a structure that extends, without permission, over a property line, easement boundary or building setback line.

Encumbrance: Any right to, or interest in, real property held by someone other than the owner, but which will not prevent the transfer of fee title (i.e. a claim, lien, charge or liability attached to and binding real property).

Environmental Impact Statement: Documents that are required by federal and state laws to accompany proposals for major projects and programs that will likely have an impact on the surrounding environment.

Equity: The fair market value of an asset less any outstanding indebtedness or other encumbrances.

Escalation Clause: A clause in a lease which provides for the rent to be increased to reflect changes in expenses paid by the landlord such as real estate taxes, operating costs, etc. This may be accomplished by several means such as fixed periodic increases, increases tied to the Consumer Price Index or adjustments based on changes in expenses paid by the landlord in relation to a dollar stop or base year reference.

Estoppel Certificate: A signed statement certifying that certain statements of fact are correct as of the date of the statement and can be relied upon by a third party, including a prospective lender or purchaser. In the context of a lease, a statement by a tenant identifying that the lease is in effect and certifying that no rent has been prepaid and that there are no known outstanding defaults by the landlord (except those specified).

Escrow Agreement: A written agreement made between the parties to a contract and an escrow agent. The escrow agreement sets forth the basic obligations of the parties, describes the monies (or other things of value) to be deposited in escrow, and instructs the escrow agent concerning the disposition of the monies deposited.

Exclusive Agency Listing: A written agreement between a real estate broker and a property owner in which the owner promises to pay a fee or commission to the broker if specified real property is leased during the listing period. The broker need not be the procuring cause of the lease.

Expense Stop: An agreed dollar amount of taxes and operating expense (expressed for the building as a whole or on a square foot basis) over which the tenant will pay its prorated share of increases. May be applied to specific expenses (e.g., property taxes or insurance).

Face Rental Rate: The "asking" rental rate published by the landlord.

Fair Market Value: The sale price at which a property would change hands between a willing buyer and willing seller, neither being under any compulsion to buy or sell and both having reasonable knowledge of the relevant facts. Also known as FMV.

Finance Charge: The amount paid for the privilege deferring payment of goods or services purchased, including any charges payable by the purchaser as a condition of the loan.

First Generation Space: Generally refers to new space that is currently available for lease and has never before been occupied by a tenant. See also "Second Generation Space.

First Mortgage: The senior mortgage, which, because of its position, has priority over all junior encumbrances. The holder of the first or senior mortgage has a priority right to payment in the event of default.

First Refusal Right or Right of First Refusal (Purchase): A lease clause giving a tenant the first opportunity to buy a property at the same price and on the same terms and conditions as those contained in a third party offer that the owner has expressed a willingness to accept.

First Refusal Right or Right of First Refusal (Adjacent Space): A lease clause giving a tenant the first opportunity to lease additional space that might become available in a property at the same price and on the same terms and conditions as those contained in a third party offer that the owner has expressed a willingness to accept. This right is often restricted to specific areas of the building such as adjacent suites or other suites on the same floor.

Fixed Costs: Costs, such as rent, which do not fluctuate in proportion to the level of sales or production.

Flex Space: A building providing its occupants the flexibility of utilizing the space. Usually provides a configuration allowing a flexible amount of office or showroom space in combination with manufacturing, laboratory, warehouse distribution, etc. Typically also provides the flexibility to relocate overhead doors. Generally constructed with little or no common areas, load-bearing floors, loading dock facilities and high ceilings.

Floor Area Ratio (FAR): The ratio of the gross square footage of a building to the land on which it's situated. Calculated by dividing the total square footage in the building by the square footage of land area.

Force Majeure: A force that cannot be controlled by the parties to a contract and prevents said parties from complying with the provisions of the contract. This includes acts of God such as a flood or a hurricane or, acts of man such as a strike, fire, or war.

Foreclosure: A procedure by which the mortgagee ("lender") either takes title to or forces the sale of the mortgagor's ("borrower") property in satisfaction of a debt. See also "Deed In Lieu Of Foreclosure."

Full Recourse: A loan on which an endorser or guarantor is liable in the event of default by the borrower.

Full Service Gross Rent: An all-inclusive rental rate that includes operating expenses and real estate taxes for the first year. The tenant is generally still responsible for any increase in operating expenses over the base year amount. See also "Pass Throughs."

Future Proposed Space: Space in a proposed commercial development that is not yet under construction or where no construction start date has been set. Future Proposed projects include all those projects waiting for a lead tenant, financing, zoning, approvals, or any other event necessary to begin construction. Also may refer to the future phases of a multi-phase project not yet built.

General Contractor: The prime contractor who contracts for the construction of an entire building or project, rather than just a portion of the work. The general contractor hires subcontractors, (e.g., plumbing, electrical, etc.), coordinates all work, and is responsible for payment to subcontractors.

General Partner: A member of a partnership who has authority to bind the partnership. A general partner also shares in the profits and losses of the partnership. See also "Limited Partnership."

Graduated Lease: A lease, generally long term in nature, which provides that the rent will vary depending upon future contingencies, such as a periodic appraisal, the tenant's gross income, or simply the passage of time.

Grant: To bestow or transfer an interest in real property by deed or other instrument, either the fee or a lesser interest, such as an easement.

Grantee: One to whom a grant is made.

Grantor: The person making the grant.

Gross Absorption: A measure of the total square feet leased over a specified period with no consideration given to space vacated in the same geographic area during the same time period. See also "Net Absorption."

Gross Building Area: The total floor area of the building measuring from the outer surface of exterior walls and windows and including all vertical penetrations (e.g. elevator shafts, etc.) and basement space.

Gross Lease: A lease in which the tenant pays a flat sum for rent out of which the landlord must pay all expenses such as taxes, insurance, maintenance, utilities, etc.

Ground Rent: Rent paid to the owner for use of land, normally on which to build a building. Generally, the arrangement is that of a long- term lease (e.g. 99 years) with the lessor retaining title to the land.

Guarantor: One who makes a guaranty. See also "Guaranty."

Guaranty: Agreement whereby the guarantor undertakes collaterally to assure satisfaction of the debt of another or perform the obligation of another if and when the debtor fails to do so. Differs from a surety agreement in that there is a separate and distinct contract rather than a joint undertaking with the principal. See also "Guarantor."

Hard Cost: The cost of actually constructing the improvements (i.e. construction costs). See also "Soft Cost."

Highest and Best Use: The use of land or buildings, which will bring the greatest economic return over a given time, which is physically possible, appropriately supported, financially feasible.

High Rise: In the Central Business District, this could mean a building higher than 25 stories above ground level but in suburban sub-markets, it generally refers to buildings higher than seven or eight stories.

Hold Over Tenant: A tenant retaining possession of the leased premises after the expiration of a lease.

HVAC: The acronym for "Heating, Ventilating, and Air-Conditioning."

Improvements: In the context of leasing, the term typically refers to the improvements made to or inside a building but may include any permanent structure or other development, such as a street, sidewalk, utilities, etc. See also "Leasehold Improvements." See also "Leasehold Improvements" and "Tenant Improvements."

Indirect Costs: Development costs, other than material and labor costs, which are directly related to the construction of improvements, including administrative and office expenses, commissions, architectural, engineering, and financing costs.

Inventory: The total amount of rentable square feet of existing and any forthcoming space (whether it be a tenant vacating space or new buildings coming on the market), in a given category, for example, all warehouse space in a specified submarket. Inventory refers to all space within a certain proscribed market without regard to its availability or condition, and categories can include all types of leased space such as office, flex, retail and warehouse space.

Judgment: This is the final decision of a court resolving a dispute and determining the rights and obligations of the parties. Money judgments, when recorded, become a lien on real property of the defendant.

Judgment Lien: An encumbrance that arises by law when a judgment for the recovery of money attaches to the debtor's real estate. See also "Lien."

Just Compensation: Compensation, which is fair to both the owner and the public when property is taken for public use through condemnation (eminent domain). The theory is that in order to be "just," the property owner should be no richer or poorer than before the taking.

Landlord's Lien: A type of lien that can be created by contract or by operation of law. Some examples are: (1) a contractual landlord's lien as might be found in a lease agreement; (2) a statutory landlord's lien; and (3) landlord's remedy of distress (or right of Distraint), which in not truly a lien but has a similar effect. See also "Lien."

Landlord's Lien or Warrant: A warrant from a landlord to levy upon a tenant's personal property (e.g., furniture, etc.) and to sell this property at a public sale to compel payment of the rent or the observance of some other stipulation in the lease.

Lease: An agreement whereby the owner of real property (i.e., landlord/lessor) gives the right of possession to another (i.e., tenant/lessee) for a specified period (i.e., term) and for a specified consideration (i.e., rent).

Lease Agreement: The formal legal document entered into between a landlord and a Tenant to reflect the terms of the negotiations between them; that is, the lease terms have been negotiated and agreed upon, and the agreement has been reduced to writing. It constitutes the entire agreement between the parties and sets forth their basic legal rights.

Lease Commencement Date: The date usually constitutes the commencement of the term of the Lease for all purposes, whether or not the tenant has actually taken possession so long as beneficial occupancy is possible. In reality, there could be other agreements, such as an Early Occupancy Agreement, which have an impact on this strict definition.

Leasehold Improvements: Improvements made to the leased premises by or for a tenant. Generally, especially in new space, part of the negotiations will include in some detail the improvements to be made in the leased premises by landlord. See also "Tenant Improvements."

Legal Description: A geographical description identifying a parcel of land by government survey, metes and bounds, or lot numbers of a recorded plat including a description of any portion thereof that is subject to an easement or reservation.

Legal Owner: The term is in technical contrast to equitable owner. The legal owner has title to the property, although the title may actually carry no rights to the property other than as a lien. See also "Lien."

Letter of Attornment: A letter from the grantor to a tenant, stating that a property has been sold, and directing rent to be paid to the grantee (buyer). See also "Attorn."

Letter of Credit: A commitment by a bank or other person, made at the request of a customer, that the issuer will honor drafts or other demands for payment upon full compliance with the conditions specified in the letter of credit. Letters of credit are often used in place of cash deposited with the landlord in satisfying the security deposit provisions of a lease.

Letter of Intent: A preliminary agreement stating the proposed terms for a final contract. They can be "binding" or "non-binding." This is the threshold issue in most litigation concerning letters of intent. The parties should always consult their respective legal counsel before signing any Letter of Intent.

Lien: A claim or encumbrance against property used to secure a debt, charge or the performance of some act. Includes liens acquired by contract or by operation of law. Note that all liens are encumbrances but all encumbrances are not liens.

Lien Waiver (Waiver of Liens): A waiver of mechanic's lien rights signed by a general contractor and his subcontractors that is often required before the general contractor can receive a draw under the payment provisions of a construction contract. May also be required before the owner can receive a draw on a construction loan.

Like-Kind Property: A term used in an exchange of property held for productive use in a trade or business or for investment. Unless cash is received, the tax consequences of the exchange are postponed pursuant to Section 1031 of the Internal Revenue Code.

Limited Partnership: A type of partnership, created under state law, comprised of one or more general partners who manage the business and who are personally liable for partnership debts, and one or more special or limited partners who contribute capital and share in profits. However, one or more of the partners take no part in running the business and incur no liability over and above the amount contributed. See also "General Partner."

Listing Agreement: An agreement between the owner of a property and a real estate broker giving the broker the authorization to attempt to sell or lease the property at a certain price and terms in return for a commission, set fee or other form of compensation. See also "Exclusive Listing Agreement."

Long Term Lease: In most markets, this refers to a lease whose term is at least three years from initial signing until the date of expiration or renewal option.

Lot: Generally, one of several contiguous parcels of land making up a fractional part or subdivision of a block, the boundaries of which are shown on recorded maps and "plats."

Low Rise: A building with fewer than four stories above ground level.

Lump-Sum Contract: A type of construction contract requiring the general contractor to complete a building or project for a fixed cost normally established by competitive bidding. The contractor absorbs any loss or retains any profit.

Maker: One who creates or executes a promissory note and promises to pay the note when it becomes due.

Market Rent: The rental income that a property would command on the open market with a landlord and a tenant ready and willing to consummate a lease in the ordinary course of business; indicated by the rents that landlords were willing to accept and tenants were willing to pay in recent lease transactions for comparable space.

Market Study: A forecast of future demand for a certain type of real estate project that includes an estimate of the square footage that can be absorbed and the rents that can be charged. Also called "Marketability Study."

Marketable Title: A title which is free from encumbrances and could be readily marketed (i.e., sold) to a reasonably intelligent purchaser who is well informed of the facts and willing to accept such title while exercising ordinary business prudence. See also "Encumbrance."

Market Value: The highest price a property would command in a competitive and open market under all conditions requisite to a fair sale with the buyer and seller each acting prudently and knowledgeably in the ordinary course of trade.

Master Lease: A primary lease that controls subsequent leases and which may cover more property than subsequent leases. An Executive Suite operation is a good example in that a primary lease is signed with the landlord and then individual offices within the leased premises are leased to other individuals or companies.

Mechanic's Lien: A claim created by state statutes for the purpose of securing priority of payment of the price and value of work performed and materials furnished in constructing, repairing, or improving a building or other structure, and which attaches to the land as well as to the buildings and improvements thereon.

Metes and Bounds: The boundary lines of land, with their terminal points and angles, described by listing the compass directions and distances of the boundaries. Originally, metes referred to distance and bounds referred to direction.

Mid-Rise: A building with between four and eight stories above ground level although in a Central Business District, this might extend to buildings up to twenty-five stories.

Mixed-Use: Space within a building or project providing for more than one use (i.e., a loft or apartment project with retail, an apartment building with office space, an office building with retail space).

Mortgage: A written instrument creating an interest in real estate and that provides security for the performance of a duty or the payment of a debt. The borrower (i.e., mortgagor) retains possession and use of the property.

Net Absorption: The square feet leased in a specific geographic area over a fixed period-of-time after deducting space vacated in the same area during the same period. See also "Gross Absorption."

Net Lease: A lease in which there is a provision for the tenant to pay, in addition to rent, certain costs associated with the operation of the property. These costs may include property taxes, insurance, repairs, utilities, and maintenance. There are also "NN" (double net) and "NNN" (triple net) leases. The difference between the three is the degree to which the tenant is responsible for operating costs. See also "Gross Lease."

Net Rentable Area: The floor area of a building that remains after the square footage represented by vertical penetrations, such as elevator shafts, etc., has been deducted. Common areas and mechanical rooms are included and there are no deductions made for necessary columns and projections of the building. (This is by the Building Owner and Manager Association - BOMA, Standard).

Net Square Footage (S.F.): The space required for a function or staff position. Also, see "Circulation Factor and "Usable Square Footage."

Non-Compete Clause: A clause that can be inserted into a lease specifying that the business of the tenant is exclusive in the property and that no other tenant operating the same or similar type of business can occupy space in the building. This clause benefits service-oriented businesses desiring exclusive access to the building's population (i.e. travel agent, deli, etc.).

Non-Recourse Loan: A loan, which bars a lender from seeking a deficiency judgment against a borrower in the event of default. The borrower is not personally liable if the value of the collateral for the loan falls below the amount required to repay the loan.

Normal Wear and Tear: The deterioration or loss in value caused by the tenant's normal and reasonable use. In many leases, the tenant is not responsible for "normal wear and tear."

Open Space: An unimproved area of land or water, or containing only such improvements as are appropriate to the use and enjoyment of the open area, and dedicated for public or private use or enjoyment or for the use and enjoyment of owners and occupants of land adjoining or neighboring such open spaces.

Operating Cost Escalation: Although there are many variations of escalation clauses, all are intended to adjust rents by reference to external standards such as published indexes, negotiated wage levels, or expenses related to the ownership and operation of buildings. During the past thirty years, landlords have developed the custom of separating the base rent for the occupancy of the leased premises from escalation rent. This technique enables the landlord to better ensure that the "net" rent to be received under the lease will not be reduced by the normal costs of operating and maintaining the property. The landlord's definition of Operating Expenses is likely to be broad, covering most costs of operation of the building. Most landlords pass through proper and customary charges, but in the hands of an overly aggressive landlord, these clauses can operate to impose obligations, which the tenant would not willingly or knowingly accept.

Operating Expenses: The actual costs associated with operating a property including maintenance, repairs, management, utilities, taxes, and insurance. A landlord's definition of operating expenses is likely to be quite broad, covering most aspects of operating the building.

Operating Expense Escalation: Although there are many variations of operating expense escalation clauses, all are intended to adjust rents by reference to external standards such as published indexes, negotiated wage levels, or expenses related to the ownership and operation of buildings.

Parking Ratio or Index: The intent of this ratio is to provide a uniform method of expressing the amount of parking that is available at a given building. Dividing the total rentable square footage of a building by the building's total number of parking spaces provides the amount of rentable square feet per each individual parking space (expressed as 1/xxx or 1 per xxx). Dividing 1000 by the previous result provides the ratio of parking spaces available per each 1000 rentable square feet (expressed as x per 1000).

Partial Taking: The taking of part (a portion) of an owner's property under the laws of eminent domain.

Pass Throughs: Refers to the tenant's pro rata share of operating expenses (i.e. taxes, utilities, repairs) paid in addition to the base rent.

Percentage Lease: Refers to a provision of the lease calling for the landlord to be paid a percentage of the tenant's gross sales as a component of rent. There is usually a base rent amount to which "percentage" rent is then added. This type of clause is most often found in retail leases.

Performance Bond: A surety bond posted by a contractor guaranteeing full performance of a contract with the proceeds to be used to complete the contract or compensate for the owner's loss in the event of nonperformance.

Plat (Plat Map): Map of a specific area, such as a subdivision, which shows the boundaries of individual parcels of land (e.g. lots) together with streets and easements.

Power of Sale: Clause inserted in a mortgage or deed of trust giving the mortgagee (or trustee) the right and power, on default in the payment of the debt secured, to advertise and sell the property at public auction.

Precast Concrete: Concrete components (i.e. walls) of a building, which are fabricated at a plant site and then shipped to the site of construction.

Preleased: Refers to space in a proposed building that has been leased before the start of construction or in advance of the issuance of a, Certificate of Occupancy.

Prime Shell Space: This typically refers to first generation (new) space that is currently available for a tenant that has never before occupied.

Prime Tenant: The major tenant in a building or, the major or anchor tenant in a shopping center serving to attract other, smaller tenants into adjacent space because of the customer traffic generated.

Pro Rata: Proportionately, according to measure, interest, or liability. In the case of a tenant, the proportionate share of expenses for the maintenance and operation of the property. See also "Common Area" and "Operating Expenses."

Punch List: An itemized list, typically prepared by the architect or construction manager, documenting incomplete or unsatisfactory items after the contractor has notified the owner that the tenant space is substantially complete.

Quitclaim Deed: A deed operating as a release that is intended to pass any title, interest, or claim that the grantor may have in the property, but not containing any warranty or professing that such title is valid.

Raw Land: Unimproved land that remains in its natural state.

Raw Space: Unimproved "shell space" in a building.

REO (Real Estate Owned): Real estate that has come to be owned by a lender, including real estate taken to satisfy a debt. Includes real estate acquired by lenders through foreclosure or, in settlement of some other obligation.

Real Property: Land, and generally whatever is erected or affixed to the land, such as buildings, fences, and including light fixtures, plumbing and heating fixtures, or other items which would be personal property if not attached.

Recapture: (1) When the IRS recovers the tax benefit of a deduction or a credit previously taken by a taxpayer, which is often a factor in foreclosure since there is a forgiveness of debt. (2) As used in leases, a clause giving the lessor a percentage of profits above a fixed amount of rent; or in a percentage lease, a clause granting the landlord a right to terminate the lease if the tenant fails to realize minimum sales.

Recourse: The right of a lender, in the event of a default by the borrower, to recover against the personal assets of a party who is secondarily liable for the debt (e.g. endorser or guarantor).

Rehab: An extensive renovation of a building or project, which is intended to cure obsolescence of such building or project.

Renewal Option: A clause giving a tenant the right to extend the term of a lease, usually for a stated period of time and at a rent amount as provided for in the option language.

Rent: Compensation or fee paid, usually periodically (i.e. monthly rent payments, for the occupancy and use of any rental property, land, buildings, equipment, etc.

Rent Commencement Date: The date on which a tenant begins paying rent. The dynamics of a marketplace will dictate whether this date coincides with the lease commencement date or if it commences months later (i.e., in a weak market, the tenant may be granted several months free rent). It will never begin before the lease commencement date.

Rentable Square Footage: Rentable Square Footage equals the Usable Square Footage and the tenant's pro rata share of the Building Common Areas, such as lobbies, public corridors and restrooms. The pro-rata share, often referred to as the Rentable/Usable (R/U) Factor, will typically fall in a range of 1.10 to 1.16, depending on the particular building. Typically, full floor occupancy will have an R/U Factor of 1.10 while partial floor occupancy will have an R/U Factor of 1.12 to 1.16 times the Usable Area.

Rentable/Usable Ratio: That number obtained when the Total Rentable Area in a building is divided by the Usable Area in the building. The inverse of this ratio describes the proportion of space that an occupant can expect to actually utilize/physically occupy.

Rental Concession: Concessions a landlord may offer a tenant in order to secure their tenancy. While rental abatement is one form of a concession, there are many others such as: increased tenant improvement allowance, signage, and lower than market rental rates and moving allowances are only a few of the many. See also "Abatement."

Rent-Up Period: The period of time, following construction of a new building, when tenants are actively being sought and the project is approaching its stabilized occupancy.

Representation Agreement: An agreement between the owner of a property and a real estate broker giving the broker the authorization to attempt to sell or lease the property at a certain price and terms in return for a commission, set fee or other form of compensation. See also "Exclusive Listing Agreement."

Request for Proposal ("RFP"): The formalized Request for Proposal represents a compilation of the many considerations that a tenant might have and should be customized to reflect their specific needs. Just as the building's standard form lease document represents the landlord's "wish list," the RFP serves in that same capacity for the tenant.

Right of First Refusal: See "First Refusal Right."

Sale-Leaseback: An arrangement by which the owner occupant of a property agrees to sell all or part of the property to an investor and then lease it back and continue to occupy space as a tenant. Although the lease technically follows the sale, both will have been agreed to as part of the same transaction.

Second Mortgage: A mortgage on property that ranks below a first mortgage in priority. Properties may have two, three, or more mortgages, deeds of trust, or land contracts as liens at the same time. Legal sequence priority, indicated by the date of recording, determines the designation first, second, third, etc.

Second Generation or Secondary Space: Refers to previously occupied space that becomes available for lease, either directly from the landlord or as sublease space. See also "First Generation Space.

Security Deposit: A deposit of money by a tenant to a landlord to secure performance of a lease. This deposit can also take the form of a Letter of Credit or other financial instrument.

Seisen (Seizen): Possession of real property under claim of freehold estate. This term originally referred to the completion of feudal investiture by which a tenant was admitted into the feud and performed the rights of homage and fealty. Presently it has come to mean possession under a legal right (usually a fee interest). As the old doctrine of corporeal investiture is no longer in force, the delivery of a deed gives seisin in law.

Setback: The distance from a curb, property line or other reference point, within which building is prohibited.

Setback Ordinance: Setback requirements are normally provided for by ordinances or building codes. Provisions of a zoning ordinance regulate the distance from the lot line to the point where improvements may be constructed.

Shell Space: The interior condition of the tenant's usable square footage when it's without improvements or finishes. While existing improvements and finishes can be removed, thus returning space in an older building to its "shell" condition, the term most commonly refers to the condition of the usable square footage after completion of the building's "shell" construction but prior to the build out of the tenant's space. Shell construction typically denotes the floor, windows, walls, and roof of enclosed premises and may include some HVAC, electrical or plumbing improvements but not demising walls or interior space partitioning. In a new multi-tenant building, the common area improvements, such as lobbies, restrooms, and exit corridors may also be included in the shell construction. With a newly constructed office building, there will often be a distinction between improvements above and below the ceiling grid. In a retail project, all or a portion of the floor slab is often installed along with the tenant improvements to better accommodate tenant specific under-floor plumbing requirements.

Site Analysis: The study of a specific parcel of land, which takes into account the surrounding area and is meant to determine its suitability for a specific use or purpose.

Site Development: The process of installation of all necessary improvements, (i.e. installment of utilities, grading, etc.), made to a site before a building or project can be constructed upon such site.

Site Plan: A detailed plan, which depicts the location of improvements on a parcel of land, which also contains all the information required by the zoning ordinance.

Slab: The exposed wearing surface laid over the structural support beams of a building to form the floor(s) of the building or laid slab- on-grade in the case of a non-structural, ground level concrete slab.

Soft Cost: That portion of an equity investment other than the actual cost of the improvements themselves (i.e. architectural and engineering fees, commissions, etc.) and which may be tax-deductible in the first year. See also "Hard Cost."

Space Plan: A graphic representation of a tenant's space requirements, showing wall and door locations, room sizes, and sometimes includes furniture layouts. A preliminary space plan will be prepared for a prospective tenant at any number of different properties and this serves as a "test-fit" to help the tenant determine which property will best meet its requirements. When the tenant has selected a building of choice, a final space plan is prepared which speaks to all of the landlord and tenant objectives and then approved by both parties. It must be sufficiently detailed to allow an accurate estimate of the construction costs. This final space plan will often become an exhibit to any lease negotiated between the parties.

Special Assessment: Any special charge levied against real property for public improvements (e.g., sidewalks, streets, water and sewer, etc.) that benefit the assessed property.

Specific Performance: A requirement compelling one of the parties to perform or carry out the provisions of a contract into which he has entered.

Speculative Space: Any tenant space that has not been leased before the start of construction on a new building. See also "First Generation Space."

Step-Up Lease (Graded Lease): A lease specifying set increases in rent at set intervals during the term of the lease.

Straight Lease (Flat Lease): A lease specifying the same, a fixed amount, of rent that is to be paid periodically during the entire term of the lease. This is typically paid out in monthly installments.

Strip Center: Any shopping area, generally with common parking, comprised of a row of stores but smaller than the neighborhood center anchored by a grocery store.

Subcontractor: A contractor working under and being paid by the general contractor. This is a worker, often a construction specialist, such as an electrical contractor, cement contractor, etc.

Subdivision Plat: A detailed drawing, which depicts the manner in which a parcel of land has been divided into two or more lots. It contains engineering considerations and other information required by the local authority.

Subordination Agreement: As used in a lease, the tenant generally accepts the leased premises subject to any recorded mortgage or deed of trust lien and all existing recorded restrictions, and the landlord is often given the power to subordinate the tenant's interest to any first mortgage or deed of trust lien subsequently placed upon the leased premises.

Surety: One who at the request of another, and for the purpose of securing to him a benefit, voluntarily binds himself to be obligated for the debt or obligation of another. Although the term includes guarantor and the terms are commonly, though mistakenly, used interchangeably, surety differs from guarantor in a variety of respects.

Surface Rights: A right or easement granted with mineral rights, enabling the possessor of the mineral rights to drill or mine through the surface.

Survey: The process by which a parcel of land is measured and its boundaries and contents ascertained.

Taking: A common synonym for condemnation or any actual or material interference with private property rights but it's not essential that there be physical seizure or appropriation.

Tax Base: The assessed valuation of all the real property that lies within the jurisdiction of a taxing authority, which is then multiplied by the tax rate or mill levy to determine the amount of tax due.

Tax Lien: A statutory lien, existing in favor of the state or municipality, for nonpayment of property taxes, which attaches only to the property upon which the taxes are unpaid.

Tax Roll: A list or record containing the descriptions of all land parcels located within the county, the names of the owners or those receiving the tax bill, assessed values, and tax amounts.

Tenant (Lessee): One who rents real estate from another and holds an estate by virtue of a lease.

Tenant at Will: One who holds possession of premises by permission of the owner or landlord, the characteristics of which are an uncertain duration (i.e. without a fixed term) and the right of either party to terminate on proper notice.

Tenant Improvements: Improvements made to the leased premises by or for a tenant. Generally, especially in new space, part of the negotiations will include in some detail the improvements to be made in the leased premises by the landlord. See also "Leasehold Improvements," "Work letter."

Tenant Improvement ("TI") Allowance or Work Letter: Defines the fixed amount of money contributed by the landlord toward tenant improvements. The tenant pays any of the costs that exceed this amount. Also commonly referred to as "Tenant Finish Allowance.

"Time is of the Essence": Means that performance by one party within the period specified in the contract is essential to require performance by the other party.

Title: The means whereby the owner of lands has the just and full possession of real property.

Title Insurance: A policy issued by a title company after searching the title and which insures against loss resulting from defects of title to a specifically described parcel of real property, or from the enforcement of liens existing against it at the time the title policy is issued.

Title Search: A review of all recorded documents affecting a specific piece of property to determine the present condition of title.

Total Inventory: This is the total amount of square footage of a type of property (i.e. office, industrial, retail, etc.) within a geographical area, whether vacant or occupied. This normally includes owner-occupied space.

Trade Fixtures: Personal property that is attached to a structure (i.e. the walls of the leased premises) that is used in the business. Since this property is part of the business and not deemed to be part of the real estate, it's typically removable upon lease termination.

Triple Net (NNN) Rent: A lease in which the tenant pays, in addition to rent, certain costs associated with a leased property, which may include property taxes, insurance premiums, repairs, utilities, and maintenances. There are also "Net Leases" and "NN" (double net) leases, depending upon the degree to which the tenant is responsible for operating costs. See also "Gross Lease."

Turn Key Project: The construction of a project in which a third party, usually a developer or general contractor, is responsible for the total completion of a building (including construction and interior design) or, the construction of tenant improvements to the customized requirements and specifications of a future owner or tenant.

Under Construction: When construction has started but the Certificate of Occupancy has not yet been issued.

Under Contract: A property for which the seller has accepted the buyer's offer to purchase is referred to as being "under contract."

Generally, the prospective buyer is given a certain period of time in which to perform its due diligence and finalize financing arrangements. During the period of time the property is under contract, the seller is precluded from entertaining offers from other buyers.

Unencumbered: Describes title to property that is free of liens and any other encumbrances. Free and clear. See also "Encumbrances.

Unimproved Land: Most commonly refers to land without improvements or buildings but can also mean land in its natural state. See also, "Raw Land."

Use: The specific purpose for which a parcel of land or a building is intended to be used or for which it has been designed or arranged.

Usable Square Footage: Usable Square Footage is the area contained within the demising walls of the tenant space. Total Usable Square Footage equals the Net Square Footage x the Circulation Factor. Also, see: Circulation Factor and Net Square Footage.

Vacancy Factor: The amount of gross revenue that pro forma income statements anticipate will be lost because of vacancies, often expressed as a percentage of the total rentable square footage available in a building or project.

Vacancy Rate: The total amount of available space compared to the total inventory of space and expressed as a percentage. Multiplying the vacant space times 100 and then dividing it by the total inventory calculate this.

Vacant Space: Refers to existing tenant space currently being marketed for lease. This excludes space available for sublease.

Variance: Refers to permission that allows a property owner to depart from the literal requirements of a zoning ordinance that, because of special circumstances, cause a unique hardship. Included would be such things as the particular physical surroundings, shape or topographical condition of the property, and when compliance would result in a practical difficulty and would deprive the owner of the reasonable use of the property.

Warranty of Possession: This is the old "quiet enjoyment" paragraph, which of course had nothing to do with noise in and around the leased premises. It provides a warranty by landlord that it has the legal ability to convey the possession of the premises to Tenant; the landlord does not warrant that he owns the land. This is the essence of the landlord's agreement and the tenant's obligation to pay rent. This means that if the landlord breaches this warranty, it constitutes an actual or constructive eviction.

Weighted Average Rental Rates: The mean proportion or medial sum made out of the unequal rental rates in two or more buildings within a market area.

Workletter: A list of the building standard items that the landlord will contribute as part of the tenant improvements. Examples of the building standard items typically identified include: style and type of doors, lineal feet of partitions, type and quantity of lights, quality of floor coverings, number of telephone and electrical outlets, etc. The Workletter often carries a dollar value but is contrasted with a fixed dollar tenant improvement allowance that can be used at the tenant's discretion. See also Leasehold Improvements and "Tenant Improvements.

Working Drawings: The set of plans for a building or project that comprise the contract documents that indicate the precise manner in which a project is to be built. This set of plans includes a set of specifications for the building or project.

Zoning: The division of a city or town into zones and the application of regulations having to do with the structural, architectural design and intended use of buildings within such designated zone (i.e. a tenant needing manufacturing space would look for a building located within an area zoned for manufacturing).

Zoning Ordinance: Refers to the set of laws and regulations, generally, at the city or county level, controlling the use of land and construction of improvements in a given area or zone.

Glossary of Terms borrowed from several locations too many to name: Thank you to all contributors. Note that these are generally accepted terminology for our industry but that this should not be construed as legal terminology and that we are not providing legal advice. Please always consult an attorney when considering legal advice.

Made in the USA
Lexington, KY
22 March 2017